VOCABULARY SKILLS & STRATEGIES

in a Balanced Reading Program

by Dorothy Rubin, Ph.D.
The College of New Jersey

Fearon Teacher Aids

A Division of Frank Schaffer Publications, Inc.

Dedication

With love to my supportive and understanding
husband, Artie,
my precious daughters, Carol and Sharon,
my delightful grandchildren, Jennifer,
Andrew, Melissa, and Kelsey,
and my considerate and charming son-in-law, Seth.

Senior Editor: Kristin Eclov

Editor: Lisa Schwimmer Marier

Copyeditor: Janet Barker

Cover and Interior Design: RedLane Studio

Illustration: Ray Barton

Cover Illustration: Jack Lindstrom, FAB Artists

Fearon Teacher Aids products were formerly manufactured and distributed by American Teaching Aids, Inc., a subsidiary of Silver Burdett Ginn, and are now manufactured and distributed by Frank Schaffer Publications, Inc. FEARON, FEARON TEACHER AIDS, and the FEARON balloon logo are marks used under license from Simon & Schuster, Inc.

© Fearon Teacher Aids

A Division of Frank Schaffer Publications, Inc.
23740 Hawthorne Boulevard
Torrance, CA 90505-5927

FE7966
ISBN 0-7682-0044-X

Contents

Contents

About This Resource

Vocabulary Skills and Strategies in a Balanced Reading Program is intended to be a valuable resource for parents and the classroom teacher by providing a wealth of challenging and stimulating vocabulary activities for young students. The wide variety of material found in this resource will help parents and classroom teachers as they work with students of all ability levels. *Vocabulary Skills and Strategies in a Balanced Reading Program* is published in a format that includes practice pages that are easily reproducible for distribution to children in classrooms or at home —an important time-saver for busy parents and teachers.

The skills and strategies presented in *Vocabulary Skills and Strategies in a Balanced Reading Program* deal with reasoning with verbal concepts and word meanings—these are the two major abilities that are the basis for solid reading comprehension. Comprehension involves thinking. As there are various levels in the hierarchy of thinking, so are there various levels of reading comprehension. Higher levels of comprehension would obviously include higher levels of thinking. This book concentrates on vocabulary skills which are often neglected in schools—and all students need help in acquiring these abilities.

This book is based on the premise that primary-grade children can and should be exposed to high-level comprehension skills at their individual literacy levels. As noted educator Jerome Bruner said in his book *The Process of Education* (Cambridge, MA: Harvard University Press, 1963), "Any subject can be taught effectively in some intellectually honest form to any child at any stage of development." While Bruner contends that this is a bold statement, there is little evidence to contradict it—and there is considerable evidence to support it. In the primary grades, children should be learning comprehension skills and strategies concomitantly with decoding and vocabulary expansion skills, and these skills should be presented in a meaningful context. The material that the children are reading should be interesting and related as closely as possible to what the children are learning. Reading is a thinking act, and unless children comprehend what they are reading, they are not *really* reading.

Whom This Guide Is For

The material in *Vocabulary Skills and Strategies in a Balanced Reading Program* is designed for students in the primary grades (K–3), but can be used with older students as well. The emphasis in this resource is on engaging children in activities that will help them become good, strategic readers.

Recent studies suggest strongly that "reading skill may not be developed as quickly or as well in the primary grades as is believed," and that "we are just beginning to detect the dire consequences that a poor initial start with reading has on later development." (From Connie Juel's "Beginning Reading" in *Handbook of Reading Research*, Volume II, Rebecca Barr, Michael L. Kamil, Peter Mosenthal, and P. David Pearson, eds., New York: Longsman 1991, p. 759.) *Vocabulary Skills and Strategies in a Balanced Reading Program* can help ensure that students are learning the vocabulary skills and strategies they need to become good readers and ultimately succeed in school.

If you are a teacher or parent with highly able children, you will find *Vocabulary Skills and Strategies in a Balanced Reading Program* a helpful teaching tool as well. The material provides the kind of challenges in vocabulary development that gifted children need and enjoy.

Each book in this series helps raise students' test scores in a variety of areas. It can help students improve their scores on standardized achievement and basic skills tests, as well as on teacher-generated tests.

Vocabulary Skills and Strategies in a Balanced Reading Program and *Comprehension Skills and Strategies in a Balanced Reading Program,* as well as the *Phonics: Skills and Strategies in a Balanced Reading Program* series helps students achieve better in school in all subject-matter areas. All of these books also start students on the road to preparing for the Scholastic Assessment Test (SAT).

The Organization

Vocabulary Skills and Strategies in a Balanced Reading Program is divided into two sections:

Section One: Vocabulary Expansion Skills

Section Two: Fun with Words: Word Riddles and Word Puzzles

Section One contains three special vocabulary skills and strategies with many practices to help students attain the skills. Each skill and strategy area includes accompanying teaching material and student practice sheets. The teaching material precedes the practices and contains the following:

Explanation
Teaching Strategies in Action
    Sample Practices
    Modeling Strategy
Learning Objective

Directions for Student Practices
Extensions
Assessment Tool Progress Report

The extensions in the teaching materials are intended to extend learning in each of the skill areas. Feel free to use some or all of them as is appropriate for your students.

The Assessment Tool Progress Report, as well as the practice exercises, are reproducible. The teaching material offers suggestions for record keeping and can be especially helpful for student portfolios.

The student practices for each skill and strategy are graduated in levels of difficulty. The beginning exercises are easier, the following are more difficult. You can, therefore, choose appropriate exercises based on the ability level of each student. The progression from easier to more difficult allows each student initial success in working with the material. Clear and understandable directions are provided for each exercise. For some exercises, when necessary, special teaching instructions are provided.

Section Two, Fun with Words, contains 88 word riddles and word puzzles that students will find interesting, enjoyable, and challenging.

Some Suggestions for Use

Vocabulary Skills and Strategies in a Balanced Reading Program can be used in various settings with a variety of students. Regardless of the program you currently embrace, *Vocabulary Skills and Strategies in a Balanced Reading Program* can help you stay aware of your students' individual differences as you continue to learn more about their reading behaviors.

I encourage you to continuously assess your children's vocabulary development. You can gain information about your students' vocabulary development using observation and student portfolios, as well as when appropriate, informal and formal diagnostic measures. You can then use this data to either reinforce, supplement, enrich, or develop skill and strategy areas using material from *Vocabulary Skills and Strategies in a Balanced Reading Program*.

The material in each book can be used in working with individual children, in small groups, or with an entire class.

What Is a Balanced Reading Program?

A balanced reading program is one in which the best of whole language practices and a sequential development of skills are fully integrated. In such a program, teachers, and parents integrate various aspects of the best of the whole language movement with different programs to achieve a balanced, eclectic approach that is also practical.

In a balanced reading program, the emphasis is on helping students improve their higher-order thinking skills, as well as gain needed comprehension and word recognition skills and strategies. In such a program, teachers also nurture a love of books in their students to help them become lifelong readers.

What Is the Role of the Teacher in a Balanced Reading Program?

Teachers are the key to the success of any program. Good teachers are aware of the individual differences of students in their classrooms, the interrelatedness of reading with the other language arts, and they understand their role in the teaching of reading.

In a balanced reading program, you, the teacher, are the key decision-maker. You determine which materials, practices, skills, and strategies to use based on the individual needs of your children. In a balanced reading program, teachers use trade books, children's writings, newspapers, textbooks, and all other appropriate materials as springboards for children's listening, speaking, reading, writing, and viewing .

Scenario: Ms. Hall in Action

Ms. Hall has been teaching reading to young children for over 30 years. She started teaching right out of college and prides herself on keeping abreast of her field. She especially enjoys noticing new trends and comparing them to the approaches she has used in her teaching over the years.

Ms. Hall loves to teach. This is evident in her relationships with her students and by what takes place in her classroom. When you ask Ms. Hall what excites her about teaching, she says, "Nothing can outdo the joy of knowing that you have taken children by the hand and helped them unlock the mystery of reading. What can be more exciting than seeing veiled eyes suddenly sparkle with a gleam that says 'I understand'? How many other careers are there that can bring such rewards each day?"

Ms. Hall has a group of 25 first graders in her classroom. She is fortunate to have a teacher's aide with whom she works very closely. At the beginning of every year, Ms. Hall spends the first few weeks getting to know her students and establishing a non-threatening environment in her classroom where creativity can flourish and students are not afraid to be risk-takers.

During the first few weeks of school, Ms. Hall helps her students establish certain routines and procedures so they can live together in harmony. She encourages suggestions from the children. She also trains her teacher's aide to be more than an assistant. She helps her teacher's aide gain the strategies and skills she needs to help with direct instruction.

Ms. Hall engages her students in many activities in an attempt to gain as much information about her students as she can gather. She also establishes a classroom portfolio system where each child has a folder and in this folder the child stores samples of his or her work-in-progress.

Ms. Hall combines the data from her students' folders with observation and informal and formal tests to organize a program for her students. She knows all her students need to have many, many opportunities to read and write, positive feedback, direct instruction based on their needs, encouragement, and lots of on-task activities. During the school day, Ms. Hall works with the whole class, with individual children, and with small groups of students.

Ms. Hall uses a combination of soft-cover trade books and other reading materials and various approaches to help her students get the most from their reading. Whether she is using a basal reader or a trade book, she employs a directed or guided reading and thinking activity. She also uses the children's experiences to develop language experience stories that they write and read together.

If you were to enter Ms. Hall's first-grade classroom a few months into the school year, you would be greatly impressed with her students' activities. Let's spend part of a day with Ms. Hall in her balanced reading program.

Ms. Hall begins each day with a special poem that she shares with the class. Today she is reading aloud Amy Lowell's poem, "City of Falling Leaves," because today is a windy fall day and leaves of all colors are falling to the ground. After she reads the poem, she engages the children in a lively discussion about autumn and falling leaves. Ms. Hall asks the children whether all trees lose their leaves in the fall. "When you go home today," she says, "check to see if there are any trees that still have their leaves. We'll talk about these tomorrow."

© Fearon Teacher Aids FE7966

Just then, a child raises his hand and says that he has lived in another part of the world where trees do not lose their leaves in the fall. He also says that the weather where he used to live almost never changes. Ms. Hall goes to the globe and points to the country where Stephan once lived before he and his family came to the United States. Ms. Hall tells the children that she spoke to Stephan and his mother and that next week Stephan's mother will come to school to talk about Stephan's homeland.

Ms. Hall says, "Stephan and his mother are coming to school to talk about the country Stephan and his family once lived in. I thought it would be a good idea if we learned something about the country first, so I went to the library and took out some books that have stories about the country Stephan is from. Then we can come up with some questions to ask Stephan and his mother. What do you think it would be like to live in a country that almost always has the same weather? Would it change your life? We'll talk about the questions later today."

Ms. Hall next invites her students to help in the general planning of the day's activities. This is what the class schedule looks like:

Reading groups
Reading aloud to children
Writing stories
Fun with words
Math (working with money—setting up a grocery store)
Lunch
Writing stories
Social studies unit
Storytelling
Creative drama
Special activities
Television reviews

Ms. Hall thanks her students for their help. She then calls a group of students to an area of the room for a small-group instructional unit. (While Ms. Hall is working with the group of students, her teacher's aide is seated in another part of the room surrounded by the rest of the children. The teacher's aide is reading aloud to the other students. She encourages predictions about what she is reading and asks questions before, during, and after.)

Ms. Hall shows her small group of children a nest with a little cloth hen sitting inside it. Ms. Hall asks the children where they think they might find chickens. A discussion ensues about farms and the kinds of animals children would find there. Ms. Hall asks if the children know what a female chicken is called. When a child says, "A hen," Ms. Hall says, "Good," and prints the word *hen* on the chalkboard. She then has the children generate a number of words using the *en* word family. First, she has them change the initial consonant to form new words. Then she has them change the final consonant. Ms. Hall puts each new word in a sentence. Ms. Hall asks the children for some other word families they have worked with before.

Ms. Hall then prints the following words on the board:

flour	wheat
bread	grain
mill	plant

After Ms. Hall helps the children gain the vocabulary words, she helps them place each new word in a sentence. She then tells the children they will be reading a story about a little red hen who has three friends. Ms. Hall explains that at the end of the story, the children will find out what kind of friends the little red hen has.

As the children read, Ms. Hall observes the children's reading behavior. Each time the children finish reading a section silently, she asks them to answer some questions. For example, Ms. Hall asks the children what they think the little red hen will do with the wheat. She asks why the little red hen's wheat grew so well. Then she asks the children to find the clues in the story that help them answer these questions and to read the clues aloud.

Throughout the story, Ms. Hall sets purposes for the silent and oral reading and has children make predictions about what they are reading. Before the children come to the end of the story, Ms. Hall asks the children to think about how they would end the story. She writes the children's predictions on paper. Ms. Hall then has the children read the final page in the book to find out what really happens. She then has the children compare their endings with the story's ending. The amount of time Ms. Hall spends on this lesson is based on the attention span and ability levels of the children.

After all the children have returned to their seats, Ms. Hall and the teacher's aide play a game of "Simon Says" with the children. They have a short recess and then Ms. Hall calls the next group to the reading table while the teacher's aide reads aloud to the other group.

Strategies to Help Children Build Their Vocabulary

The emphasis in this book is on providing direct instruction to the children. *Direct instruction* is instruction guided by a teacher who uses various strategies or techniques to help children gain reading skills. There are a number of strategies teachers can use to teach reading directly. The strategies that you use should not be affected by the kinds of materials you use. In other words, one teacher may use only trade books in his or her class, while another might use a basal reader. Both can employ similar strategies to help students gain needed concepts. As stated previously, this text advocates a mix of materials, beliefs, and strategies.

Special Note

A *strategy* is a systematic plan for achieving a specific objective or result.
An *instructional reading strategy* is the action or actions that a teacher takes to help children gain reading skills.

Interactive Instruction

In interactive instruction, the teacher intervenes at optimal times to improve instruction. The teacher determines when to intervene and what materials and strategies to use to achieve the desired learning for the readers with whom she or he is working.

Modeling Instruction

Modeling instruction requires teachers to think out loud. That is, teachers verbalize their thoughts to help students "see" an appropriate strategy or reading behavior. This is an exceptionally effective strategy because it helps students gain insight into the kind of thinking involved in reading comprehension and helps children recognize that reading comprehension is analogous to problem solving.

Interactive instruction combined with modeling and knowledge of questioning techniques at various levels is very effective in helping students find meaning in what they are reading.

Scenario: Ms. Hall Uses a Modeling Strategy with Her First Graders

Ms. Hall and seven children are working together at the reading table. They have been reading the story, "The Hare and the Tortoise." Ms. Hall has discussed with the children what a hare and a tortoise are. She has shown the children pictures of both and talked about which animal they would expect to move faster and why. She has gone over all new or unfamiliar words in the story with the children, and before they began to read the story, she had asked the children to make predictions about who they thought would win the race.

Today Ms. Hall has asked the children to do something a little different. They are going to be detectives. After discussing what a detective does, Ms. Hall asks the children to look for clues in the story to show why the hare lost the race.

She rereads the story with the children before she shows them how to find story clues. Then she says, "While I am reading the first two pages of the story, I see something that tells me the rabbit is very sure of himself. I think to myself that this will probably get him into trouble. Hare said, 'Rabbits run fast as the wind.' I don't think he took Tortoise very seriously. Hare feels it's silly to think that Tortoise could possibly win. Because of this, Hare feels he can take it easy. Now, everyone look at the next page. Are there any clues there that show us that the hare could lose the race?"

Ms. Hall calls on different children and elicits from them the reasons for their choices. When they have finished giving all their clues, Ms. Hall asks the children if they have ever heard the saying, "Slow and steady wins the race." She asks the children to think about what this means. Later, she says, they will discuss this.

Vocabulary Development and Semantic Mapping (Graphic Organizer)

Semantic mapping is a technique that has become more and more popular because it seems to help students gain the concepts they need to better comprehend their reading material. Semantic mapping stresses word meanings and categorizing—two major elements for concept development.

There is no one set pattern for semantic mapping, however, a few steps are usually followed. First, the teacher chooses a word or topic that is related to what the students are reading about or studying. The word is put in a central position on the chalkboard. Next, the children are asked to brainstorm as many words as they can think of that are related to the word on the board. The children's words are put on the board in categories. Then the teacher asks the students to work by themselves and write on a sheet of paper as many words as they can generate that are related to the central word. The teacher also suggests that they group their words. The teacher then encourages the students to share their lists. As the children do this, the teacher writes the words in categories on the chalkboard. (This procedure does not usually take too long because there are generally many duplications.) In addition, the teacher adds words to the list.

© Fearon Teacher Aids FE7966

After all the words are recorded on the chalkboard, the teacher asks the children to suggest labels for the various groups of words. Finally, the teacher and children discuss the listed words and how they are labeled, paying special attention to all new words.

Here is a scenario that illustrates how one teacher uses semantic mapping with her second-graders:

Mrs. Smith's class will begin a new unit on various types of animals. She has broken the unit into a number of manageable parts and has perused the children's textbook, as well as some other materials they will be reading. From the readings, she has chosen a few terms related to the topic and based on the level and needs of her students. One of the terms she has chosen is pets. She would like to determine the background information that her students have on this concept. (She knows that relating past information or experiences to present information or experiences is necessary for comprehension.) She does not want to take anything for granted. As she would like them to write stories about pets, a semantic mapping exercise would be very helpful.

Mrs. Smith explains to the children that before they begin the new unit, she would like to go over some key words with them. She puts the word *PETS* in uppercase letters in the center of the board and asks the children to state all the words that they can think of related to the word *pets*.

Mrs. Smith writes the words in categories on the board as the children state them. Here is what the chalkboard looks like at this point:

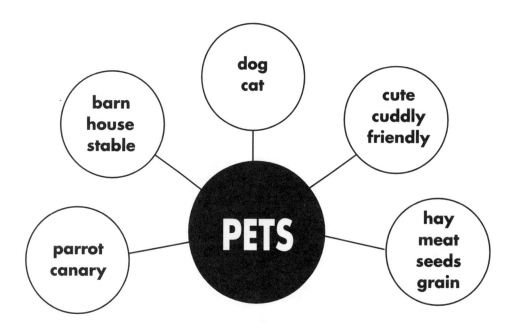

Next, the children are told to list on a sheet of paper any other words they can think of related to the word *pets* and to group the words so that those things that belong together are together. (The children have worked with categorizing before.)

After a while, Mrs. Smith asks the children to share their lists and then to add labels to the lists of words on the board. A finished semantic map follows. (Mrs. Smith added the words *chirp, groom, grain,* and *caress.*)

Mrs. Smith and her students discuss the words and how they are grouped. She pays particular attention to the words she added and any others she feels some children may not know. They also discuss how the words can be categorized in a number of different ways. In addition, the teacher makes sure the children note that the words *pet, groom,* and *train* have different meanings based on their position in the sentence.

Example of a Vocabulary Lesson Plan

Objectives

1. The children will be able to give words that best describe the sense of touch portrayed in a number of presented pictures.
2. The children will be able to give the opposites of words relating to touch.
3. The children will be able to state words to fit the blanks of sentences read aloud by the teacher.

Preliminary Preparation

1. Pictures depicting the sense of touch
2. Two pictures—one portraying a small clown and the other showing a large clown
3. A rose in a vase
4. Sentences to be read aloud by the teacher:
   a. The sandpaper feels very _____.
   b. The cactus plant feels very _____.
   c. The chalkboard feels very _____.

Introduction

"Let's review some of the things we've been working with. We've been working with words that sound just like the sound they make. We've been working with our five senses. What are they? Very good. Sight, touch, smell, hearing, and taste. We've also been working with words that are opposites. Look at this picture. What do you see? Yes, a very big clown. Look at this picture. What do you see? Good, a very little clown. What is different about these two pictures? Good, in one the clown is little, and in the other the clown is big. What do we call these words? Yes, opposites. Today we will put together some of the things we've been working with. We will combine opposites with the sense of touch."

Development

"Let's look at this picture. What do you see? Yes, a little girl falling off her tricycle. Do you think the little girl hurt herself? Yes, she probably did. How do you know this? Good, because she is riding on the sidewalk. How do you think the sidewalk feels? Yes, *rough*, *scratchy*, and *hard*. I'll put these words on the board. Now, let's look at this picture. What do you see? Yes, a little boy who fell on the grass. Do you think the little boy hurt himself? I agree, he probably didn't. Why not? Very good, because the grass is *soft*. I'll put the word *soft* on the chalkboard. Let's look at these two pictures. What do you see? Yes, one picture shows a girl riding her bicycle on a bumpy road, and another picture shows a boy riding his bicycle on a smooth road. Which is easier to ride on? I agree. Let's put the words *smooth* and *bumpy* on the board."

The teacher then picks up the vase on her desk, which contains a rose with thorns. She asks some children to touch the petals very, very gently and then to tell how they feel. She writes what they say on the board. She asks some other children to touch the stem with thorns gently and to say how that feels. She writes what they say on the board.

The teacher repeats all the words on the board. She asks the children to give her words that are opposites. After this, she reads aloud the three sentences with missing words. She asks the children to supply a word that would make sense in the sentence. A number of words could fit. The word does not have to be one from the board.

Summary

The teacher elicits from the students what they did today. She helps them to pull the main points of the lesson together.

Forward Look

She then tells them tomorrow they will be working with words that have to do with smell.

Section One: Vocabulary Expansion Skills

Developing Vocabulary Expansion Skills

Good vocabulary and good reading skills go hand in hand. Unless children know the meaning of words, they will have difficulty in understanding what they are reading. Without an understanding of words, reading comprehension is impossible.

As children advance in concept development, their vocabulary development must also advance—the two are interrelated. Children deficient in vocabulary will usually be deficient in concept development. That's why it is so important to build children's sight vocabulary as well as stress the vocabulary development that concerns the building of a larger word-meaning vocabulary. Studies have shown that vocabulary is not only a key factor in reading comprehension but also a major component of most aptitude tests.

Vocabulary Development and Individual Differences

For a vocabulary program to be successful, individual differences must be recognized among the amount and kinds of words that kindergarten and first-grade children have in their listening vocabulary (ability to understand a word when it is spoken). Some children come to school with a rich and varied listening vocabulary, whereas others have a more limited and narrow vocabulary. Some children may come to school with a rich and varied vocabulary that can be used with their peers and at home, but it may not be one that is very useful to them in school. For example, some children may possess a large lexicon of street vocabulary and expressions, and some others may speak a dialect of English that may contain its own special expressions and vocabulary.

Be aware that a young child's listening vocabulary is larger than his or her speaking vocabulary and certainly larger than his or her reading and writing vocabulary. All four areas of vocabulary need to be developed. However, because a child first learns language through the aural-oral approach, begin with the listening and speaking areas first.

Vocabulary Consciousness

In the primary grades, children begin to come across words that are spelled the same but have different meanings based on their context in the sentence. For example, children learn that the word *saw* in "I *saw* Eddie" does not carry the same meaning as it does in "Sarah helped her dad *saw* the wood." When primary-grade children recognize that *saw, train, coat,* and many other words have different meanings based on surrounding words, children are beginning to build a *vocabulary consciousness.* This vocabulary consciousness grows when children begin asking about and looking up new words that they come across in their everyday activities.

As students become more advanced in reading, their vocabularies can be expanded in fun ways. One way to challenge primary-grade level children's budding vocabulary consciousness is to use word riddles or word activities (see Section Two). If children are fascinated with words, they will want to know the largest word in the dictionary, enjoy doing word games and puzzles, and have fun pronouncing funny or nonsense-sounding words. Help children to do the following:

1. Become aware of words they do not know.
2. Try to guess the meanings of words from the context.
3. Begin to learn word parts.
4. Jot down words that they do not know and look the words up in the dictionary later.
5. Keep a notebook and write down the words they have missed in their vocabulary exercises.
6. Maintain interest in wanting to expand vocabulary.

The practices in this book concern the building of vocabulary. A brief explanation of the vocabulary expansion skills that are present in this section follows:

Skill 1	Using Context Clues to Determine Word Meanings	To figure out the meaning of a word from the surrounding words in the sentence.
Skill 2	Expanding Vocabulary with Words That Have the Same or Nearly the Same Meaning (Synonyms) and Words That Are Opposite in Meaning (Antonyms)	To find and understand the difference in words that have the same or similar meanings (synonyms) and words that are opposite in meaning (antonyms).
Skill 3	Expanding Vocabulary Using Words with Multiple Meanings (Homographs)	To figure out the meaning of words that are spelled the same but have different meanings based on how they are used in the sentence.

Skill 1:

<u>Using Context Clues to Determine Word Meanings</u>

Explanation

Context clues help students determine the meanings of unfamiliar words. By context, we mean the words surrounding a word that can throw light on its meaning. A context clue is an item of information surrounding a particular word in the form of a definition, description, explanation, comparison, contrast, example, synonym, antonym, and so on.

Help students be aware of the various clues that writers give readers to understand the meaning of less familiar words. Some textbook writers will define, describe, or explain a word to make sure that readers understand the meaning. Other techniques that writers use include comparison and contrast, synonyms and antonyms, examples, and more.

Teaching Strategies in Action

Help your students use context clues to figure out word meanings. Explain to the children that context clues are helpful in figuring out unfamiliar words in sentences. Share with the children that context clues are especially important in figuring out words with multiple meanings. Present the following sentence to the children and see if they can figure out the meaning of the word *enormous.*

Example:
Jane's house was so *enormous* that we got lost in it.

From the context of the sentence, children should realize that the word *enormous* must mean "large" or "very big."

Sometimes children can actually determine the definition of a word from the sentence or from sentences that follow.

Example:
Darryl behaved in a very *rash* manner. He rushed in too quickly and was not very careful.

From the sentences, children should determine that the word *rash* refers to something that is done too quickly and not very carefully.

Alert readers can also use contrasts or comparisons to gain clues to meanings of words. Have your students try to determine the meaning of the word *prudent* in the following sentence:

Example:

Mary is usually a *prudent* person, but she was foolish yesterday.

If your students guessed *wise* for the meaning of *prudent*, they were correct. Students learn from the context clues that the word *prudent* is somehow the opposite of the word *foolish*. This is an example of contrasts.

In the next sentence, your students can see how comparisons can help them figure out the meaning:

Example:

Fred was as *obstinate* as a mule.

In this sentence, the word *obstinate* means "stubborn." A mule is an animal that is considered stubborn. By understanding the comparison, your students can get an idea of what *obstinate* means, even though it is a difficult word or one that they may not have seen before.

In the following sentence, your students can see how examples can help them figure out the meaning of a word:

Example:

The only *tools* I have are a hammer, saw, and wrench.

From the examples, *hammer, saw,* and *wrench,* your students learn that a tool must be an instrument that you use to fix or make something.

In the following sentence, your students can see how the words *that is* signal that an explanation is to follow:

Example:

The story is incredible—*that is,* it is simply not believable.

Help your students to recognize that good readers use all these clues to help them determine word meanings.

Sample Practices

Here are some sample practices that you can use with your students:

1. The eagle *soared* over the tall trees.
   An eagle flies and these trees are tall, so the word *soared* must mean "to fly high."

2. Wanda wasn't very *considerate*. She wasn't thoughtful of the feelings of others.
   The word *considerate* means to be thoughtful of the feelings of others.

The second sentence gives the clue.

3. Peter is as funny as a *comedian*.

Peter is funny and Peter is as funny as a comedian, so the word *comedian* must mean a funny person.

4. I was famished—*that is*, I was very hungry.
The words *that is* let students know there is an explanation—*famished* means "very hungry."

Modeling Strategy

Here is how Ms. Schneider helps the children learn to use context clues. She presents her students with the following sentences:

Mrs. Brown grows vegetables on her farm.
She grows peas, beans, corn, carrots, and beets.

Then Ms. Schneider says, "Here is how I go about figuring out the meaning of the word *vegetables*. From reading the sentences, I see that there are a number of clues to help me figure out the meaning of the word *vegetables*. The clues are *peas, beans, corn, carrots*, and *beets*. The words *peas, beans, corn, carrots*, and *beets* are examples of vegetables. I know that examples are not the meaning of a word. An example is something that shows what the rest are like. Examples may not be the meaning of a word, but they can help us figure out word meanings. From the examples, I see that vegetables are parts of plants that we eat."

Then she says, "Here are two other sentences. Let's see if we can figure out the meaning of the word *family* using examples as clues." Ms. Schneider puts the following two sentences on the chalkboard:

There are six people in my family.
My grandmother, mother, father, two brothers, and I live in our home.

"See if you do the same things I do. First, I look for the clues. The clues are *six people, grandmother, mother, father, two brothers*, and *I*. The sentences do not give me the meaning of the word *family*, but they give me examples. The words *grandmother, mother, father, brothers*, and *I* are all examples and part of a family. Usually, families live together in the same home. From these examples, I see that these people are part of a family. They are all related and live together in the same home."

Learning Objective

To use a variety of context clues to determine the meanings of words.

Directions for Student Practices

Use the student practices on pages 26-40 to help your students acquire, reinforce, and review using context clues to determine word meanings. Pick and

© Fearon Teacher Aids FE7966

choose the practices based on the needs and developmental levels of your students. Answers for the student practice pages are on page 152.

When practicing using context clues to determine word meanings, have the children read the directions and then answer the questions. For those who have difficulty reading, read the directions aloud to the children and orally ask them the questions.

For Practices 12-15, which deal with scrambled words in stories, you might want to give children a list of the words correctly spelled in alphabetical order. This added aid will help children in unscrambling the scrambled words in the story. Of course you can adjust any direction to accommodate the individual differences of your students.

Extensions

What Do You Think?
Encourage students to make note of new words in their reading that they have never seen before. Ask students to write definitions of the words based on the context clues. (You many want to preselect the words.) Then invite students to compare their definitions with definitions in the dictionary.

Vocabulary Challenge
Have each student find an unfamiliar word in their reading. Ask each student to first read the word aloud to the class, and then read the word in the context of the sentence. Invite the other students to decide if the meaning can be determined from the context, and, if so, what the meaning is. You may want to do this in small groups, especially if you have a wide range of reading abilities.

Vocabulary Quilt
Invite each child to choose a vocabulary word from a favorite story or book that they would like to illustrate. Provide squares of paper or muslin in whatever size you prefer, keeping in mind how large you want the finished quilt to be. Invite each child to write his or her vocabulary word on a square. Encourage children to also illustrate their vocabulary words with colorful markers. Help children write sentences using their vocabulary words as part of their designs. If you use paper squares, the squares can be taped to a large sheet of colored butcher paper and displayed on a wall in the classroom. If you use muslin, you can sew each child's design together to make a quilt.

Student's Name _____

Assessment Tool Progress Report

Progress

Improvement

Comments

Name _____

Practice 1

Directions: Read each sentence carefully. Use context clues to help you choose the word that best fits the sentence. Write the word in the blank. All the words in the word list are used as answers.

Word List: rose, point, suit, box, play

1. That was a good _____ she made in the game.

2. The pitcher stood in the _____.

3. We _____ late yesterday.

4. That color does not _____ you.

5. What is the _____ of the story?

Name _____

Practice 2

Directions: Read each sentence carefully. Use context clues to help you choose the word that best fits the sentence. Write the word in the blank. All the words in the word list are used as answers.

Word List: run, rest, pitch, bear, strike

1. It was _____ black last night.

2. The movie will _____ for two weeks.

3. The workers went on _____.

4. Leave the _____ for me.

5. Tell them to _____ left.

© Fearon Teacher Aids FE7966
Reproducible

Name _____

Practice 3

Directions: Read each sentence carefully. Use context clues to help you choose the word that best fits the sentence. Write the word in the blank. All the words in the word list are used as answers.

Word List: iron, monkey, lamb, plum, plant

1. My father works in a _____.

2. What a _____ that job is. It is so easy.

3. They tricked the man and made a _____ out of him.

4. He is as tame as a _____.

5. They will try to _____ out the problems.

Name _____

Practice 4

Directions: Read each sentence carefully. Use context clues to help you choose the word that best fits the sentence. Write the word in the blank. All the words in the word list are used as answers.

Word List: broke, break, fast, pinch, flowed

1. During the _____, I met my friend.

2. On Fridays, I am always _____.

3. The crowd _____ through the gate.

4. I always feel the money _____ on Fridays.

5. After being on a _____, I was starved.

Name _____

Practice 5

Directions: Read each sentence carefully. Use context clues to help you choose the word that best tells how the person in the sentence feels. Write the word in the blank. All the words in the word list are used as answers. A word may be used only once.

Word List: sad, sick, tired, good, silly

1. When my kitten was hurt, I felt _____.

2. Jake felt _____ when he saw that he was wearing one red sock and one blue sock.

3. After eating too much, Jack felt _____.

4. Carol felt _____ when she was invited to the party.

5. Serena was _____ after working hard all day.

Name _____

Practice 6

Directions: Read each sentence carefully. Use context clues to help you choose the word that best tells how the person in the sentence feels. Write the word in the blank. All the words in the word list are used as answers. A word may be used only once.

Word List: angry, ashamed, proud, happy, insulted

1. Sharon was _____ when she saw a big boy hitting a little boy.

2. Chad was _____ when his sister won a prize.

3. Leanne was _____ when she was not invited to the party.

4. Greg was _____ that he had lied to his best friend.

5. Arthur was _____ when his parents bought him a bicycle.

© Fearon Teacher Aids FE7966
Reproducible

Name _____

Practice 7

Directions: Read each sentence carefully. Use context clues to help you choose the word that best tells how the person in the sentence feels. Write the word in the blank. All the words in the word list are used as answers. A word may be used only once.

Word List: embarrassed, guilty, peculiar, scared, joyful

1. Teresa was _____ when the sleeve of her dress tore when she raised her arm.

2. Bob was _____ when he saw the big dog coming toward him.

3. Lisa felt _____ when all her tests were over.

4. Bart felt _____ about leaving all the work for the others to do.

5. Jim felt _____ about the situation and didn't know how to act.

Name _____

Practice 8

Directions: Read each sentence carefully. Use the context clues to help you figure out the meaning of the underlined word. Sometimes the clue to the word meaning is in the second sentence. Write the meaning of the underlined word in the blank.

1. It is <u>difficult</u> for me to climb a rope. _____

2. It seemed <u>incredible</u> that he could do all that work in one hour. _____

3. Jennifer will play a <u>dual</u> role in the play. She will play both a child and an old lady. _____

4. The doctors said that they had no quick <u>remedy</u> for the child's illness. _____

5. The material was so <u>coarse</u> that it hurt my skin.

_____

Name _____

Practice 9

Directions: Read each sentence carefully. Use the context clues to help you figure out the meaning of the underlined word. Sometimes the clue to the word meaning is in the second sentence. Write the meaning of the underlined word in the blank.

1. My kitten is very <u>tame</u>. She will not hurt anyone. _____

2. Everyone knows her, because she is a <u>famous</u> writer.

   _____

3. That is such an <u>enormous</u> ice-cream cone. You will have to eat some of it. _____

4. We can all walk side by side on that street because it is 10 feet <u>broad</u>. _____

5. The lion is a <u>fierce</u> animal. _____

6. The elephant is a <u>huge</u> animal. _____

7. The <u>valiant</u> knight fought the dragon. _____

8. The medicine was so <u>potent</u> that it knocked out a six-foot-tall man. _____

9. After the fire <u>demolished</u> their house, the Browns had no place to live. _____

10. Mr. Smith gave both boys <u>equivalent</u> jobs to do. They both had to take care of the plants. _____

Name _____

Practice 10

Directions: Each sentence contains a nonsense word. Read each sentence carefully. Choose a word that you think makes sense in place of the nonsense word. Write the word in the blank. You may choose any word you like. The word, however, must make sense in the sentence.

1. I like to <u>freble</u> _____ with my kitten.

2. My father took us on a <u>booble</u> _____ ride.

3. On the farm, we saw a <u>deeble</u> _____ sitting on her eggs.

4. Next <u>fromen</u>, _____ we are going to visit my grandmother.

5. My <u>greib</u> _____ and I are going swimming.

6. At the <u>loim</u>, _____ we saw a funny-looking animal.

7. Who <u>grammed</u> _____ that?

8. I like to <u>drebe</u> _____.

9. <u>Wurit</u> _____ is my favorite food.

10. At the <u>hoteim</u>, _____ we are not allowed to do that.

Name _____

Practice 11

Directions: Each sentence contains a nonsense word. Read each sentence carefully. Choose a word that you think makes sense in place of the nonsense word. Write the word in the blank. You may choose any word you like. The word, however, must make sense in the sentence.

1. My brother, <u>Sentle</u>, _____ and I went to the beach.

2. No one wants to <u>liert</u> _____ anymore.

3. At <u>verter</u>, _____ we have lots of fun.

4. After school, we played <u>meint</u> _____.

5. When I'm hot, I go <u>reinting</u> _____.

6. Please <u>neim</u> _____ that for me.

7. <u>Leiper</u> _____ helped the poor little dog.

8. A <u>brite</u> _____ was stuck in the tree.

9. The <u>hert</u> _____ is coming to town soon.

10. The <u>poiter</u> _____ frightened me.

© Fearon Teacher Aids FE7966
Reproducible

Name _____

Practice 12

Directions: The following is a short story with scrambled words. Read each sentence carefully. Use context clues to help you figure out the scrambled words. Unscramble the words and write the correct words in the blanks below the story.

The Mouse in the House

I have a mouse that lives in my house. The <u>soume</u>[1] that lives <u>ni</u>[2] my house <u>si</u>[3] very <u>msatr</u>.[4] I like <u>ti</u>.[5] I <u>vegi</u>[6] it <u>hescee</u>[7] to eat. I <u>lpay</u>[8] <u>dehi</u>[9] and <u>eeks</u>[10] with it. I like <u>hte</u>[11] mouse that lives in my <u>seouh</u>.[12]

1. _____   7. _____

2. _____   8. _____

3. _____   9. _____

4. _____   10. _____

5. _____   11. _____

6. _____   12. _____

Name _____

Practice 13

Directions: The following is a short story with scrambled words. Read each sentence carefully. Use context clues to help you figure out the scrambled words. Unscramble the words and write the correct words in the blanks below the story.

The Cat in the Tree

One day my cat ran up a tree. It <u>saw</u>[1] a very big <u>reet</u>.[2] My <u>tac</u>[3] sat on a <u>rbacnh</u>[4] of the tree. She <u>tas</u>[5] and <u>tas</u>[6] and <u>tas</u>.[7] We tried <u>ot</u>[8] get her to come <u>nwod</u>.[9] She just said "<u>eowm</u>."[10] She sat in the <u>reet</u>[11] all <u>ghtin</u>.[12] In the <u>nomring</u>,[13] <u>hes</u>[14] still sat in the tree. We did <u>ton</u>[15] know <u>htaw</u>[16] to do. Just then, <u>ew</u>[17] heard a <u>oudl</u>[18] noise. It frightened <u>ym</u>[19] cat. She <u>nar</u>[20] down the tree.

1. _____

2. _____

3. _____

4. _____

5. _____

6. _____

7. _____

8. _____

9. _____

10. _____

11. _____

12. _____

13. _____

14. _____

15. _____

16. _____

17. _____

18. _____

19. _____

20. _____

Name _____

Practice 14

Directions: The following is a short story with scrambled words. Read each sentence carefully. Use context clues to help you figure out the scrambled words. Unscramble the words and write the correct words in the blanks below the story.

Making New Friends

It is hard for me to make new friends. I am a hys[1] person. I ma[2] also very quiet. On[3] one really notices em.[4] I never know hawt[5] to yas.[6] In hscool[7] I never raise my dahn.[8] I verne[9] keasp.[10] I do ton[11] like to eb[12] shy. I am not evry[13] happy. I would like to vahe[14] lots of refinds.[15]

1. _____   9. _____

2. _____   10. _____

3. _____   11. _____

4. _____   12. _____

5. _____   13. _____

6. _____   14. _____

7. _____   15. _____

8. _____

Name _____

Practice 15

Directions: The following is a short story with scrambled words. Read each sentence carefully. Use context clues to help you figure out the scrambled words. Unscramble the words and put the correct words in the blanks below the story.

The Animal Cookie

 One day a little girl baked a little cookie. The keicoo[1] was a funny ttleil[2] bunny. It dah[3] gib[4] ears and a cute little lait.[5] The little grli[6] liked her cookie. Just sa[7] she saw[8] about to eat her little ynnbu,[9] she heard a voice yas[10] "Little girl, do ton[11] tea[12] me. Please od[15] not eat em."[14] The little lirg[15] looked around. There was on[16] one there. "Oolk[17] at me. Look ta[18] me," the voice said. The little girl deoolk[19] at the ooceik.[20] The cookie was inglatk![21] "I won't tea[22] you," said the little girl. Just then hte[23] little bunny hopped off the batle[24] and pohped[25] away. The little girl nar[26] after the cookie, tub[27] she could not tacch[28] the cookie. The nnuby[29] was too saft[30] for her.

1. _____	11. _____	21. _____
2. _____	12. _____	22. _____
3. _____	13. _____	23. _____
4. _____	14. _____	24. _____
5. _____	15. _____	25. _____
6. _____	16. _____	26. _____
7. _____	17. _____	27. _____
8. _____	18. _____	28. _____
9. _____	19. _____	29. _____
10. _____	20. _____	30. _____

Skill 2:

Expanding Vocabulary with Words That Have the Same or Nearly the Same Meaning (Synonyms) and Words That Are Opposite in Meaning (Antonyms)

Explanation

Synonyms and antonyms are often used by writers to enhance their writing. A *synonym* is a word with the same or nearly the same meaning. An *antonym* is a word that is opposite in meaning. By teaching children about synonyms and antonyms through examples as well as through the context of their own reading, you can help expand children's vocabulary significantly.

Because synonyms and antonyms are excellent context clues that writers use often, a special section is devoted to these two very important clues.

Teaching Strategies in Action

Synonyms are words that have the same or nearly the same meaning. Often, words may be defined by other words that are similar in meaning. The similar word that is used is often a word that is more familiar or more commonly used.

Examples:
> *Indolent* is defined as "lazy."
> *Dire* is defined as "extreme."
> *Famished* is defined as "starved."
> *Valiant* is defined as "brave."

Antonyms are words opposite in meaning to others. Often, words may also be defined by other words of opposite and more familiar meaning.

Examples:
> *Reluctant* is the opposite of "willing."
> *Significant* is the opposite of "unimportant."
> *Complex* is the opposite of "simple."

Help your students recognize that writers use synonyms and antonyms to make their writing clearer, more expressive, more informative, and more interesting.

Sample Practices

Here are some sample practices that you can use with your students.

Have your students generate either synonyms or antonyms for the underlined words in the sentences below:

1. The boat <u>drifted</u> on the water.
   Synonym: floated

2. Sheila <u>invented</u> a new dance.
   Synonym: created

3. Barbara was very <u>loud</u>.
   Antonym: quiet

4. Paul turned <u>up</u> the music.
   Antonym: down

Modeling Strategy

Here is how Mrs. Green helps her students use antonyms and synonyms to figure out word meanings. Mrs. Green has worked with the children to understand the concept of opposites. The children can give her the opposites of *tall, big, high, hard, thin, cruel,* and many other words as well. Mrs. Green puts the following sentence on the chalkboard and asks her students to tell her the meaning of the word *intelligent*:

Andrew is *intelligent but* his pal Jim is dumb.

"Here is what I do to figure out the meaning of the word *intelligent*," Mrs. Green says. "I read the sentence. I notice the word *but*. The word *but* is a signal that a contrast or an opposite follows. I know what the word *dumb* means. *Dumb* means "not smart." The opposite of *intelligent* is "not smart." Therefore, the word *intelligent* must mean "smart."

Mrs. Green presents her students with another sentence and has the children try to figure out the meaning of *gloomy*.

Yesterday it was *gloomy* out *but* today it is a *bright* day.

Children should be able to state that the word *gloomy* is the opposite of the word *bright*; therefore, *gloomy* means not "bright" but "dark."

Mrs. Green also helps the children figure out word meanings using words with similar meanings (synonyms). She writes the following sentence on the chalkboard that contains an unfamiliar word. Mrs. Green then verbalizes her thoughts in figuring out the meaning of the unfamiliar word.

Sharon said that she felt ill after eating *rancid or* spoiled food.

Mrs. Green says, "I see the word *or* in the sentence. Often the word *or* is used by the writer when he or she uses another word with a similar meaning. I don't know what the word *rancid* means, but I do know what the word *spoiled* means. It means "rotten" or "bad." *Spoiled* is similar in meaning to *rancid*. So *rancid* must mean "spoiled." (If the term *rancid* is used with your upper primary-grade children, make sure they understand that we talk about *rancid food*. Tell children that the term *rancid* does not refer to people.)

Learning Objective

To find words that have the same or nearly the same meaning as well as words with opposite meanings.

Directions for Student Practices

Use the student practices on pages 46–55 to help your students acquire, reinforce, and review synonyms and antonyms. Pick and choose the practices based on the needs and developmental levels of your students. Answers for the student practice pages are on pages 152–153.

When practicing synonyms and antonyms, have the children read the directions and then answer the questions. For those who have difficulty reading, read the directions aloud to the children and orally ask them the questions.

Extensions

Make a Game

Divide the class into small groups and have each group design a simple game board based on a favorite story or book. Each game board should include a trail with a start and finish. Have children mark spaces throughout the trail with the words *synonym* and *antonym*. Write vocabulary words on cards. Students can use spinners or dice to determine how many spaces to move. A player spins or rolls the dice and moves the number of spaces indicated. He or she then takes the top vocabulary card and reads it aloud. If he or she has landed on a *synonym* space, then he or she must think of a synonym for the vocabulary word. The same is true for spaces marked *antonym*. The first player to reach the finish wins.

Finding Synonyms and Antonyms

Encourage students to look for sentences in their reading that use pairs of synonyms or antonyms in the same sentence. Have students write the sentences on long strips of paper and then pin the strips on a bulletin

© Fearon Teacher Aids FE7966

board. Then invite students to take turns finding synonyms or antonyms in the sentences written by their classmates.

Synonym and Antonym Pillows

Invite children to select synonym or antonym pairs to illustrate on pillows. Provide large muslin squares for the pillows. Provide markers, fabric paints, or fabric crayons for the illustrations. (Using fabric paints or fabric crayons will make the pillows washable. Follow the directions on the box.) Give each child two pieces of muslin—one for each word in their pairs of synonyms or antonyms. Encourage children to illustrate each of the words in the pair—one word on each piece of muslin. Help children put the illustrated sides of the fabric together and hand-stitch or machine-sew around three sides. Then show the children how to turn the fabric right-side out and stuff the inside with batting. Help children sew the openings closed.

Student's Name _____

Assessment Tool Progress Report

Progress

Improvement

Comments

Name _____

Practice 1

Directions: Read each sentence carefully. Then read the words in the word list. Choose a word from the word list that is the same or almost the same as the underlined word in each sentence. Write the word in the blank. All the words in the word list are used as answers.

Word List: joyful, bright, ill, handsome, big

1. That is a <u>large</u> house. _____

2. The baby is <u>sick</u>. _____

3. He is a <u>happy</u> man. _____

4. I like <u>smart</u> people. _____

5. Scott is <u>good-looking</u>. _____

Name _____

Practice 2

Directions: Read each sentence carefully. Then read the words in the word list. Choose a word from the word list that is the same or almost the same as the underlined word in each sentence. Write the word in the blank. All the words in the word list are used as answers.

Word List: mean, lady, thin, little, correct

1. The <u>small</u> dog is cute. _____

2. Your answer is not <u>right</u>. _____

3. She is a <u>nasty</u> person. _____

4. The <u>woman</u> wore a blue outfit. _____

5. Jim is too <u>skinny</u>. _____

Name _____

Practice 3

Directions: Read each sentence carefully. Then read the words in the word list. Choose a word from the word list that is the same or almost the same as the underlined word in each sentence. Write the word in the blank. All the words in the word list are **not** used as answers.

Word List: cut, rope, rip, place, picture, spirit, price, game, ripe, pal, stuck, struck, spend, champ

1. What is the <u>cost</u> of that? _____

2. My <u>friend</u> is very nice. _____

3. I have a big <u>tear</u> in my sleeve. _____

4. He <u>hit</u> the ball hard. _____

5. That is a beautiful <u>spot</u>. _____

Name _____

Practice 4

Directions: Read each sentence carefully. Then read the words in the word list. Choose a word from the word list that is the same or almost the same as the underlined word in each sentence. Write the word in the blank. All the words in the word list are **not** used as answers.

Word List: healthy, worthy, many, bright, finish, wealthy, moist, dry, dump, poor

1. My friend is <u>rich</u>. _____

2. That was a <u>smart</u> thing to do. _____

3. That is <u>damp</u>. _____

4. I hope my dog is <u>well</u>. _____

5. We will <u>end</u> the game soon. _____

Name _____

Practice 5

Directions: Read each sentence carefully. Then read the words in the word list. Choose a word from the word list that is the same or almost the same as the underlined word in each sentence. Write the word in the blank. All the words in the word list are **not** used as answers.

Word List: dark, dull, damage, end, near, start, aid, chum, brother, scent, perfume, wide, trouble, hold, bottom, head, defend, star, line, clever

1. She is a <u>bright</u> student. _____

2. Let's <u>begin</u> the game now. _____

3. He is a good <u>buddy</u>. _____

4. My cat is at the <u>top</u> of the stairs. _____

5. My friend needs <u>help</u>. _____

6. When will you <u>finish</u> the game? _____

7. I will try to <u>protect</u> you. _____

8. That is a lovely <u>odor</u>. _____

9. What <u>harm</u> did the dog do to the house? _____

10. Did you go to a lot of <u>effort</u> to do that? _____

Name _____

Practice 6

Directions: Read each sentence carefully. Then read the words in the word list. Choose a word from the word list that is opposite in meaning to the underlined word in the sentence. Write the word in the blank. All the words in the word list are used as answers.

Word List: low, tall, back, little, later

1. He is a <u>short</u> man. _____

2. The kitten is <u>big</u>. _____

3. That is too <u>high</u>. _____

4. The teacher will talk to you <u>now</u>. _____

5. That is the <u>front</u> of the dress. _____

© Fearon Teacher Aids FE7966
Reproducible

Name _____

Practice 7

Directions: Read each sentence carefully. Then read the words in the word list. Choose a word from the word list that is opposite in meaning to the underlined word in the sentence. Write the word in the blank. All the words in the word list are used as answers.

Word List: beautiful, clean, asleep, good, well

1. I feel <u>sick</u>. _____

2. He is a <u>bad</u> puppy. _____

3. The room is <u>dirty</u>. _____

4. The picture is <u>ugly</u>. _____

5. She is <u>awake</u>. _____

Name _____

Practice 8

Directions: Read each sentence carefully. Then read the words in the word list. Choose a word from the word list that is opposite in meaning to the underlined word in the sentence. Write the word in the blank. All the words in the word list are used as answers.

Word List: guilty, old, empty, sad, stale

1. She is <u>happy</u>. _____

2. The drawer is <u>full</u>. _____

3. That bat is <u>new</u>. _____

4. That bread is <u>fresh</u>. _____

5. She is <u>innocent</u>. _____

53

Name _____

Practice 9

Directions: Each sentence below has two missing words. The missing words are opposite in meaning. Complete each sentence with word opposites that make sense in the sentence.

Example:

If you eat too much, you may become too ____**fat**____.

but if you eat too little, you may become too __**thin**__.

1. A giant is _____, but a dwarf is _____.

2. Sandpaper is _____, but cotton is _____.

3. When you play a game, you want to _____ not _____.

4. When the sun _____, it's dawn, and when the sun _____, it's dusk.

5. The rain makes you _____, and the sun makes you _____.

Name _____

Practice 10

Directions: Each sentence below has four missing words. The missing words are two pairs of word opposites. Read the words in the word list. Complete each sentence with word opposites from the word list that make sense in the sentence. All the words in the word list are **not** used as answers.

Word List: kind, play, awake, never, love, asleep, night, happy, always, day, hate, sad, help, sister, father, aunt, cousin, bad, brother, hurt, weak, cry, stay, healthy, pay, strong, niece, sick, laugh, cruel

Example: John is _____**sad**_____ when he _____**loses**_____ a game, but he is __**happy**_____ when he _____**wins**_____.

1. You may _____ when you are _____, and you may _____ when you are _____.

2. You are usually _____ during the _____, and you are usually _____ during the _____.

3. You are _____ when you are _____, and you are _____ when you are _____.

4. When you are _____, people _____ you but when you are _____, people _____ you.

5. My _____ is _____ late, but my _____ is _____ late.

© Fearon Teacher Aids FE7966

Skill 3:

Expanding Vocabulary Using Words with Multiple Meanings (Homographs)

Explanation

Words that are spelled the same but have different meanings are called *homographs*. Because many words have more than one meaning, you should help students recognize that the meaning of a particular word is determined by its use in a sentence.

Some homographs are spelled the same but do not sound the same.

Example:

1. During the garbage strike, there were tons of uncollected *refuse* on the streets of the city.

2. I *refuse* to go along with you.

The word *refuse* means "trash." The word *refuse* also means "to decline to accept." In sentence 1, *refuse* (ref' use), meaning "trash," is pronounced differently from the term *refuse* (rē fuse'), meaning "to decline to accept" in sentence 2. In reading, you can determine the meaning of *refuse* from the way it is used in the sentence (context clues).

To avoid confusion, all of the practices in this section will present words with multiple meanings that are spelled the same and sound the same. These homographs are easier for children to work with.

> **Special Note**
>
> You may want to use the term *words with multiple or many meanings* with the students rather than *homographs*. You might introduce the term *homograph* to some of your older students.

Teaching Strategies in Action

Because many words have more than one meaning, the meaning of a particular word is determined by the position (syntax) of the word in a sentence and from meaning (semantic) clues of the surrounding words. Tell your students that they must be careful to use words with multiple meanings correctly.

Example:

"It wasn't *fair* that Harry got to go to the *fair* and I didn't."

Here, the word *fair* is spelled the same and sounds the same. But the meaning of the word *fair* is different in each case.

Sample Practices

Here are some sample practices that you can use with your students.

1. Use of the word *present*:
   a. Terry brought a *present* to Josh's birthday party.
   b. Phil was *present* at the meeting.

   Explain to students that in the first sentence, the word *present* means "gift." In the second sentence, it means "at hand" or "in existence."

2. Use of the word *spring*.
   a. *Spring* is finally here!
   b. Joanne walks with a *spring* in her step.

   Point out to children that the word *spring* in the first sentence refers to the season. *Spring* in the second sentence means "bounce" or "step lightly."

Modeling Strategy

Here is how Mr. Dupre helps the children work with words with multiple meanings (homographs). He writes the following pairs of sentences on the chalkboard:

1. The dogs *bark* at night.
2. The *bark* of the tree is peeling.

1. The *train* had a lot of people in it.
2. Did you *train* your dog to do that?

Mr. Dupre then says, "What do you notice about these sentences? I notice that there are two sets of sentences. In each set, there is one word that is spelled the same. However, when I read each sentence in the set, I see that the same word means something different in each sentence. Let me see, in the first sentence of the first set, the word *bark* is an action word (a verb). It tells what the dog is doing. It tells what sound the dog is making. In the second sentence, the word *bark* is a naming word (a noun). It refers to the tough outer covering of a tree."

Mr. Dupre continues. "Now in the second set of words, I see that *train* is a naming word in the first sentence. It is a connected line of railroad cars that brings people from one place to another. In the second sentence, *train* is an action word. It means 'to teach.'"

"It's the other words in the sentences that help me figure out the correct meanings of the words *bark* and *train*. The position of *bark* and *train*—that is, where each word is in the sentence—helps me figure out the meaning of each word."

Mr. Dupre then invites the children to practice working with words with multiple meanings. "Now that you have seen how I figure out the meanings of words that are spelled the same, here are some practices that will challenge you to do the same. Later on, we can make up some word riddles using words that are spelled the same but have different meanings."

Learning Objective

To figure out the meanings of words that are spelled the same but have different meanings based on how each word is used in the sentence.

Directions for Student Practices

Use the student practices on pages 61–70 to help your students acquire, reinforce, and review words with multiple meanings (homographs). Pick and choose the practices based on the needs and developmental levels of your students. Answers for the student practice pages are on page 153.

When practicing using words with multiple meanings, have the children read the directions and then answer the questions. For those who have difficulty reading, read the directions aloud to the children and orally ask them the questions.

Special Note

The presented homograph practices can be done in small groups or with the entire class, as well as individually. If children work individually on the homograph practices, it would help to go over the answers together in a group to encourage discussion and interaction.

Extensions

Two-Faced Puzzles

Invite each child to illustrate a word with multiple meanings on an 8 1/2" x 11" (21.25 cm x 27.5 cm) posterboard. On the other side of the posterboard, he or she can illustrate another meaning for the word. Then help each child cut the illustrated posterboard into puzzle pieces. Store each puzzle in a plastic resealable bag. Write the word illustrated on a piece of masking tape and label each bag.

Concentration Card Game

Have students write down words with multiple meanings they encounter in their reading. Provide blank index cards for the children and invite them to illustrate each word on two separate cards, using one meaning of the word on one card and the other meaning of the word on the other card. Then have children include an appropriate caption for each card using the word in a sentence. For example, using the word *plant*, a child may want to draw a plant on one card with the sentence, "This is my green *plant*." On the other card, he or she might draw a picture of the plant in a garden with the sentence, "I think I will *plant* my *plant* in my garden." Then children can use the sets of words with multiple meanings for a concentration card game. Place sets of cards, in scrambled order, face down on a table or the floor.

Each player, in turn, flips two cards up. If they make a set of words with multiple meanings, they keep these cards. If not, the cards are turned face down again, and it's the next person's turn. The winner is the child with the most card sets.

Funny Stories and Silly Poems

Invite students to make lists of words with multiple meanings that they find in their reading. Each child can then make a "word bank" of homographs to use to write funny stories or silly poems. Display stories and poems in the classroom.

Student's Name _____

Assessment Tool Progress Report

Progress

Improvement

Comments

Name _____

Practice 1

Directions: Read each sentence carefully. Choose a word from the word list that fits the blanks of the sentence and makes sense. Each word in the word list has different meanings but is spelled the same. All the words in the word list are used as answers. The first is done for you.

Word List: fall, train, pet, bark, can

Example: I <u>can</u> carry that heavy <u>can</u> of beans.

1. My dog will _____ if you pick the _____ off the tree.

2. I need to _____ my dog not to bark when he hears the

   _____.

3. During the _____, the leaves begin to _____ in some

   parts of the country.

4. My _____ doesn't like you to _____ it too much.

Name _____

Practice 2

Directions: Read each sentence carefully. Choose a word from the word list that fits the blanks of the sentence and makes sense. Each word in the word list has different meanings but is spelled the same. All the words in the word list are used as answers. The first is done for you.

Word List: fan, swing, well, spring, plant

Example: It's fun to <u>swing</u> on the <u>swing</u>.

1. In the _____, I saw a fish _____ out of the _____.

2. The cat didn't feel _____ when it fell in the _____ and got all wet.

3. We will _____ a _____ in our yard that will grow very tall.

4. On a hot day, I use my little _____ to _____ myself.

Name _____

Practice 3

Directions: Read each sentence carefully. Choose a word from the word list that fits the blanks of the sentence and makes sense. Each word in the word list has different meanings but is spelled the same. All the words in the word list are **not** used as answers. The first is done for you.

Word List: trail, march, saddle, grade, farm, tree, groom, fair, pass, pat, park, case, four

Example: I needed a <u>pass</u> to <u>pass</u> through the gate.

1. The _____ said that he would _____ the horse for

   his bride.

2. My mother wanted to _____ the car and then go for a

   walk in the _____.

3. I am in third _____ and I always get a good _____ in

   social studies.

4. We went to the _____ on a _____ day and we had

   lots of fun there.

Name _____

Practice 4

Directions: Read each sentence carefully. Choose a word from the word list that fits the blanks of the sentence and makes sense. Each word in the word list has different meanings but is spelled the same. All the words in the word list are **not** used as answers.

Word List: play, help, show, team, well, fine, group, band, ring, spell, batted, hit, class, glass

1. We needed to _____ our tickets to get into the _____.

2. My father did not feel _____ when he paid the parking _____.

3. The witch put a _____ on anyone who could not _____.

4. When he _____ a home run, he made a _____ with the fans.

5. The person in the _____ wore a _____ around his head when he played the piano.

Name _____

Practice 5

Directions: Read each sentence carefully. Choose a word from the word list that fits the blanks of the sentence and makes sense. Each word in the word list has different meanings but is spelled the same. All the words in the word list are **not** used as answers.

Word List: flower, cap, pitch, rose, pin, point, run, skip, jack, sock, hose, show

1. My sister _____ early in the morning to water her

   _____.

2. The garden _____ made my mother's _____ wet.

3. The teacher used a stick with a sharp _____ to

   _____ something out to us.

4. My brother used a _____ to _____ up his car.

5. When the mower refused to _____, I had to _____ to

   the store to buy a part for it.

Skill 3: Expanding Vocabulary Using Words With Multiple Meanings (Homographs)

Name _____

Practice 6

Directions: Read each sentence carefully. Think of a word that is spelled the same but has different meanings that fits the blanks of the sentence and makes sense. Write the word in the blanks. The first is done for you.

Example: Everyone <u>present</u> received a <u>present</u>.

1. The _____ in the pond likes to _____ its head in

   the water.

2. Use the _____ to _____ together the torn hem.

3. My new _____ had a _____ of paint on its sleeve.

4. The gold _____ is _____ and it will make me very rich.

Name _____

Practice 7

Directions: Read each sentence carefully. Think of a word that is spelled the same but has different meanings that fits the blanks of the sentence and makes sense. Write the word in the blanks. The first is done for you.

Example: I get a tan when I <u>sun</u> myself in the <u>sun</u>.

1. The _____ of the land said that he needed a _____ to measure something.

2. They use a multicolored _____ to _____ the race cars down when they come into the home stretch.

3. At the _____, the princess was given a large, round _____.

4. My brother will not eat _____ because he is very short, and everyone calls him a _____.

5. The children stood in _____ to buy a fishing _____.

6. He spun the _____ on _____ of the table.

7. I found a wooden _____ on my neighborhood _____ as I walked down the street.

8. I asked Sally to _____ me a _____ of paper to write the note on.

9. We put our money in the _____ close to the river _____.

Name _____

Practice 8

Directions: Read each sentence carefully. Think of a word that is spelled the same but has different meanings that fits the blanks of the sentence and makes sense. Write the word in the blanks. The first is done for you.

Example: I will <u>cart</u> the leaves away in my <u>cart</u>.

1. Don't _____ my milk _____ so much.

2. We did not _____ to be _____ to the _____ man, so we said that we were sorry.

3. As the train went over the _____, my brother and sister were playing _____.

4. We used _____ to _____ the broken paper box.

5. Many people bought tickets at the _____ office to watch the fighters _____.

6. The _____ of the tribe gave the _____ reason for not going to the meeting.

7. You are the _____ who is number _____ in the class.

8. The _____ was about children who _____ make-believe games.

Name _____

Practice 9

Directions: Read each set of sentences carefully. Think of a word that is spelled the same but has different meanings that fits each set of sentences. Write the word in the blank. The first is done for you.

Example: You weigh yourself on these. A fish has these. <u>scales</u>

1. You call pennies, nickels, and dimes this. You do this with your clothing. _____

2. You do this to an envelope. This animal lives in the water, and it can be trained to balance a ball on its nose. _____

3. You can lie on this in the water. You can do this in the water. _____

4. This is an insect. A plane does this. _____

5. You eat soup out of this. You play this sport with a large, hard ball. _____

6. You can write one of these. There are 26 of them in the alphabet. _____

7. You do this to get somewhere. You shovel this when it is covered with snow. _____

8. You wear this under a dress. If this happens, you may fall. _____

Name _____

Practice 10

Directions: Read each set of sentences carefully. Think of a word that is spelled the same but has different meanings that fits each set of sentences. Write the word in the blank.

1. A man usually wears this. You do this to a rope. _____

2. You wear these to help you see better. You can drink out of these. _____

3. A bell does this. You can wear it on your finger. _____

4. You need this if you are tired. It's what is left over. _____

5. This person plays baseball. It can hold water. _____

6. This can be a room. It's what you need to do to do well on a test. _____

7. This sometimes holds toothpaste. You can float on it in the water. _____

8. You need this to mail a letter. You can do this with your foot. _____

9. This is a baby goat. It's a child. It's also done to fool you. _____

10. This is a large bird. It's also a machine. _____

11. This is put in a lock. This is the main thing. _____

12. When you do this to your fingers, you make a noise. Clothing may have this. _____

Section Two
Fun With Words: Word Riddles and Word Puzzles

Fun with Words is a special section that your students should find challenging and enjoyable. Similar activities are grouped together and based on graduated levels of difficulty within each group. However, feel free to change the order to any sequence that will better suit the needs of your students.

The objectives for each similar group of activities state the various skills included in the groups of activities.

Learning Objectives

Activities 1–16: Word Riddles

To use reasoning ability and vocabulary skills in following directions to solve the different word riddles.

Activities 17–33: Word Puzzles

To use vocabulary skills, spelling skills, and following-direction skills to solve the various word puzzles.

Activities 34–42: Word Square Puzzles

To use visual discrimination, vocabulary skills, and spelling skills to find the required number of words or the special words in each word square puzzle.

Activities 43–52: Word Riddle Puzzles

To use visual discrimination, following-directions skills, and synthesis skills to solve each of the word riddle puzzles.

Activities 53–65: Rhyming Word Puzzles

To use auditory and/or visual discrimination and vocabulary skills to solve the rhyming word puzzles.

Activities 66–76: Scrambled Word Puzzles

To use visual discrimination, vocabulary skills, spelling skills, and synthesis skills to solve each scrambled word puzzle.

Activities 77–82: Hidden Word Puzzles

To use visual discrimination, spelling skills, vocabulary skills, and categorizing skills to solve the hidden word puzzles.

Activities 83–88: Hidden Clue Puzzles

To use visual discrimination skills, vocabulary skills, spelling skills, and categorizing skills to solve the hidden clue puzzles.

Student's Name _____

Assessment Tool Progress Report

Progress

Improvement

Comments

Name _____

Word Riddles 1

Let's go on a farm-animal hunt. Below are riddles with a word following each. If you follow directions and solve the riddle, you will discover the animals.

1. Change one of my letters, and I'll give you milk. cot _____

2. Change one of my letters, and I'll quack. luck _____

3. Change one of my letters, and I'll lay an egg. pen _____

4. Take away one of my letters, and I'll eat hay. hoarse _____

Name _____

Word Riddles 2

Lets go on a farm-animal hunt. Below are riddles with a word following each. If you follow directions and solve the riddle, you will discover the animals.

1. Change one of my letters, and I'll oink.   pit   _____

2. Change one of my letters, and I'll bark.   log   _____

3. Change one of my letters, and I'll bray.   mile   _____

4. Change one of my letters, and I'll go for a swim.   loose   _____

Name _____

Word Riddles 3

Let's go on a wild-animal hunt. Below are riddles with a word following each. If you follow directions and solve the riddle, you will discover the animals. Be careful. It's hard to find these animals.

1. Add one letter to me, and I'll climb a tree.　money　_____

2. Change two of my letters, and I'll run swiftly
   through the woods.　seed　_____

3. Change two of my letters, and I'll roar.　lime　_____

4. Change one letter, then take away one letter,
   and you'll have a striped animal.　finger　_____

Name _____

Word Riddles 4

Let's go on a wild-animal hunt. Below are riddles with a word following each. If you follow directions and solve the riddle, you will discover the animals. Be careful. It's hard to find these animals.

1. Change one letter, and you'll have a smart animal.

    box   _____

2. Change one letter, and you'll know whom Little
    Red Riding Hood met.   golf   _____

3. Change one letter, then take away one letter,
    and you'll have an animal that likes honey.

    heart   _____

4. Change one letter, then add one letter, and
    you'll have a very dangerous animal.

    father   _____

Name _____

Word Riddles 5

See how many of the word riddles you can solve.

1. I'm the opposite of **end**. Take away one of my letters, and you will
   see me on a clear night.

   _____ _____

2. I come from the sky. Add one letter to me, and you can ride away.

   _____ _____

3. This is what you do to a book. Add one letter to me, and you'll
   have something to eat.

   _____ _____

4. This is something you like to do. Take away one of my letters,
   and you'll know what hens do with eggs.

   _____ _____

Name _____

Word Riddles 6

See how many of the word riddles you can solve.

1. I'm something you eat out of. Take away one of my letters, and I'll fly away.

   _____ _____

2. I'm the opposite of **early**. Add one letter to me, and you can eat off me.

   _____ _____

3. I'm another word for **girl**. Add one letter to me, and you can drink out of me.

   _____ _____

4. I'm an insect that makes honey. Add three letters to me, and I'll become an insect that eats leaves.

   _____ _____

Name _____

Word Riddles 7

See how many of the word riddles you can solve.

1. I grow in the ground. Take away two of my letters, and I'll
   crawl all over the ground.

   _____ _____

2. I get this when I am cold. Take away two of my letters, and you'll
   know what may happen to me if I get too cold.

   _____ _____

3. I'm used as a signal in a car. Take away one of my letters,
   and I become an insect.

   _____ _____

4. I'm a female deer. Add one letter to me, and I become a
   bird of peace.

   _____ _____

Name _____

Word Riddles 8

See how many of the word riddles you can solve.

1. I'm something you do in an airplane. Add one letter to me, and you'll have an important member of a wedding party.

   _____ _____

2. I'm found in a house. Add one letter to me, and you'll have another important member of a wedding party.

   _____ _____

3. I'm an insect. Add two letters to me, and you'll also find me at the wedding.

   _____ _____

4. I'm the opposite of **thin**. Add three letters to me, and you'll also find me at the wedding.

   _____ _____

Name _____

Word Riddles 9

See how many of the word riddles you can solve.

1. I help get you to school on time. Take away one of my letters, and I'll help keep anyone out of your room.

   _____ _____

2. Plants grow in me. Add one letter to me, and you'll know what happens to meat if it stays out too long.

   _____ _____

3. You do this to leaves. Add one letter to me, and you'll have something that stops a car.

   _____ _____

4. I'm good to eat. Add one letter to me, and you may find me in an oyster.

   _____ _____

Name _____

Word Riddles 10

See how many of the word riddles you can solve.

1. I'm something that helps you row a boat. Add two letters to me, and you can write on me.

   _____ _____

2. I mean the same as **steal**. Add one letter to me, and you can wear me.

   _____ _____

3. I'm something you take when you are sick. Take away one of my letters, and you can walk on me.

   _____ _____

4. I'm a cloth you throw away. Add one letter to me and I'll boast.

   _____ _____

Name _____

Word Riddles 11

See how many of the word riddles you can solve.

1. I'm what you do when you study at the last moment for a test.
   Add one letter to me, and you'll know what you can get if you sit
   in the same position too long.

   _____ _____

2. I'm a person who tries to make your stay comfortable and pleasant.
   Add one letter to me, and I'll be able to haunt you.

   _____ _____

3. I'm a bird. Add two letters to me, and I'll become a tool that will
   help you untwist things.

   _____ _____

4. I'm found at the base of a window. Add one letter to me,
   and I'll become foolish.

   _____ _____

Name _____

Word Riddles 12

See how many of the word riddles you can solve.

1. My first word is something that you can ride in. My second word is the opposite of **out**. Put us together, and you have a place at which you can stay.

   _____ _____ _____

2. My first word means **steal**. My second word is the opposite of **out**. Put us together, and I will fly away.

   _____ _____ _____

3. My first word is another word for friend. My second word is a high card. Put us together, and you will have a very beautiful place.

   _____ _____ _____

4. My first word is something you cook in. My second word is a three-letter word that means **attempt**. Put us together, and you have a place to store things.

   _____ _____ _____

Fun With Words

Name _____

Word Riddles 13

See how many of the word riddles you can solve.

1. My first word is something that you ride in. My second word is a heavy weight. Put us together, and you have something that holds things.

   _____   _____   _____

2. My first word is part of your body. My second word is a small word that is used a lot. Put us together, and you have a covering that is worn in battle.

   _____   _____   _____

3. My first word is something you drink out of. My second word is something you can use for building. Put us together, and you have a place to store what I was drinking out of.

   _____   _____   _____

4. My first word is something you can sleep on. My second word is a heavy weight. Put us together, and you have very soft material.

   _____   _____   _____

Name _____

Word Riddles 14

Below are four sets of riddles. One word fits each set of riddles.
Find the word.

Example: I'm used at the beginning of a sentence, and I'm the seat
of government. Answer: capital

1. I'm a color, and I'm good to eat. _____

2. You can do this to animals, and you can ride in me.

   _____

3. I'm part of a tree, and dogs do this. _____

4. I'm what you do to a car, and you can play in me.

   _____

Name _____

Word Riddles 15

Below are four sets of riddles. One word fits each set of riddles.
Find the word.

1. A plant needs me to live and so does a tooth.

   _____

2. I'm good to eat, but I can cause you lots of trouble if you get

   caught in me. _____

3. I'm something a king wears on his head, and I'm also the top of

   your head. _____

4. I can head a country, and I can help you make straight lines.

   _____

Name _____

Word Riddles 16

Below are four sets of riddles. One word fits each set of riddles.
Find the word.

1. I'm a card game, and cars go over me.

   _____

2. Children play with me; I can be used to build houses, and a football
   player does this.

   _____

3. I'm a large hole, and I can be found in many fruits.

   _____

4. I can make music, and I can be worn around the arm or head.

   _____

Name _____

Word Puzzles 17

Fill in the spaces to make 10 four-letter words. To help you, a clue and a letter are given for each word.

1. Animals live in this building. ____ A ____ ____

2. Something hot can do this. ____ U ____ ____

3. You do this to leaves. ____ A ____ ____

4. You play with this. ____ A ____ ____

5. You ride this on the snow. ____ I ____ ____

6. This is the opposite of **mean**. ____ I ____ ____

7. This is another word for **ill**. ____ I ____ ____

8. This is a color. ____ I ____ ____

9. This is a wild animal. ____ O ____ ____

10. This is a bird found on a farm. ____ U ____ ____

Name _____

Word Puzzles 18

Below are 10 clues for 10 words. Each word has three letters, and the first and last letters are the same. The first is done for you.

1. A way of saying **father**.   ____dad____

2. A small child.   _____

3. A baby wears this.   _____

4. This is a way of saying **mother**.   _____

5. This is a relative.   _____

6. This is another way of saying **father**.   _____

7. This is a person who belongs to the church.   _____

8. This is a joke.   _____

9. This is a young dog.   _____

10. This is something you see with.   _____

Name _____

Word Puzzles 19

Below are five clues for five words. Use the last two letters of the word that comes before to begin the next word. The first is done for you.

1. This is an animal.   _____cat_____

2. You did this when you were hungry.   _____

3. You brush these.   _____

4. You use this in sewing.   _____

5. You do this to numbers.   _____

Word Puzzles 20

Below are six clues for six words. Use the last two letters of the word that comes before to begin the next word. The first is done for you.

1. This is a friend.   _____pal_____

2. You are this when no one is around.   _____

3. This is the opposite of **far**.   _____

4. This is a school subject.   _____

5. This makes things cold.   _____

6. This is a penny.   _____

Name _____

Word Puzzles 21

Below are seven clues for seven words. Use the last letter of the word that comes before to begin the next word. The first is done for you.

1. You read this.   ____book____

2. This unlocks something.   _____

3. This is a color.   _____

4. This is what you do to keep clean.   _____

5. This is where people live.   _____

6. This is something you hear with.   _____

7. This is a flower.   _____

Name _____

Word Puzzles 22

Below are seven clues for seven words. Use the last letter of the word that comes before to begin the next word.

1. This is the opposite of **princess**.   _____

2. This is the opposite of **start**.   _____

3. This is the opposite of **night**.   _____

4. This is the opposite of **old**.   _____

5. This is the opposite of **boy**.   _____

6. This is the opposite of **right**.   _____

7. This is the opposite of **give**.   _____

Name _____

Word Puzzles 23

Below are four clues for four words. Each word contains a smaller word that is something to eat.

1. This is a farm animal. _____

2. You do this if you are frightened. _____

3. You use this to bang in a nail. _____

4. This is a precious gem. _____

Word Puzzles 24

Below are four clues for four words. Each word contains a smaller word that is part of your body.

1. You sit in this. _____

2. This comes from your eyes. _____

3. You find animals here. _____

4. This is a nut. _____

Word Puzzles 25

Below are four clues for four words. Each word has a smaller word in it that is a number.

1. Something sweet that bears like. _____

2. Many times _____

3. Cargo _____

4. To go to a meeting _____

Name _____

Word Puzzles 26

Below are five clues for five words. Each new word uses all the letters of the word above it and also adds one letter. To make each new word, you may place the letters in any way you wish. The first is done for you.

1. This is a small word. (one letter) _____a_____

2. This is another way of saying **mother**. (two letters) _____

3. This is the opposite of **woman**. (three letters) _____

4. A lion has this. (four letters) _____

5. This is a state in the Northeast. (five letters) _____

Word Puzzles 27

Below are five clues for five words. Each new word uses all the letters of the word above it and also adds one letter. To make each new word, you may place the letters in any way you wish. The first is done for you.

1. This is a pronoun. (one letter) _____I_____

2. This is a greeting. (two letters) _____

3. This is what a baseball bat does. (three letters) _____

4. This is the opposite of **fat**. (four letters) _____

5. You do this in your mind. (five letters) _____

Name _____

Word Puzzles 28

Below are eight clues for eight words. Each new word has four letters. Start at number 1 and go on changing only one letter in each word to make a new word. The first is done for you.

1. You eat this.   <u>food</u>

2. This is the opposite of **bad**.   _____

3. This is a color.   _____

4. This is the opposite of **hot**.   _____

5. This is something that was said.   _____

6. This is something you pay to cross some bridges. _____

7. This is made out of dough.   _____

8. This is a part you can play.   _____

Name _____

Word Puzzles 29

Below are eight clues for eight words. Each word has five letters. Start at number 1 and go on changing only one letter in each word to make a new word. The first is done for you.

1. You use this to light something. _____match_____

2. You do this to a ball. _____

3. Chickens do this from eggs. _____

4. You put this on a door. _____

5. You put this on torn clothes. _____

6. A baseball player does this. _____

7. This woman is found in fairy tales. _____

8. This helps you to tell the time. _____

Name _____

Word Puzzles 30

Below are seven clues for seven words. Each word has one more letter than the one before it. Each word also begins with the next letter of the alphabet. The first is done for you.

1. A very small word.   A

2. Another small word that is used a lot.   __ __

3. This holds things.   __ __ __

4. You have this when there is no light.   __ __ __ __

5. This is the opposite of **exit**.   __ __ __ __ __

6. This is a parent.   __ __ __ __ __ __

7. You throw this out.   __ __ __ __ __ __ __

Word Puzzles 31

Below are seven clues for seven words. Each word is a three-letter word and the middle letter of the word starts with the next letter of the alphabet. The first is done for you.

1. I'm a high card in a deck of cards.   A   C   E

2. You do this to numbers.   __ __ __

3. I'm an insect.   __ __ __

4. I'm the opposite of **on**.   __ __ __

5. I tell how old you are.   __ __ __

6. I'm the opposite of **he**.   __ __ __

7. I have a sharp point.   __ __ __

Name _____

Word Puzzles 32

Below are six clues for six words. Each word begins and ends with the same letter.

    1. A lion does this.   _____

    2. You can do this to bread.   _____

    3. This is put in a lamp.   _____

    4. A bell makes this sound.   _____

    5. This is the opposite of **low**.   _____

    6. This is the opposite of **front**. _____

Word Puzzles 33

Below are five clues for five words. The first letter of the word is the same as the last letter of the word. The second letter of the word is the same as the next-to-last letter of the word.

Example: **sees**.
The letter **s** is the first and last letter of the word and the letter **e** is the second and next-to-last letter of the word.

    1. Midday.   _____

    2. To blow a horn.   _____

    3. A chick says this.   _____

    4. This is a person who likes books a lot. _____

    5. Something that is done.   _____

Name _____

Word Square Puzzle 34

Below is a word square puzzle. It has 10 color words in it. You can go across and down to find the words. See how many you can find.

```
A  D  P  G  R  A  Y
O  E  U  R  E  D  E
R  B  R  O  W  N  L
A  R  P  I  N  K  L
N  B  L  U  E  O  O
G  R  E  E  N  N  W
E  B  L  A  C  K  Y
```

1. _____   6. _____

2. _____   7. _____

3. _____   8. _____

4. _____   9. _____

5. _____   10. _____

101

Name _____

Word Square Puzzle 35

Below is a word square puzzle. It has the name of 14 things to eat and drink in it. You can go across and down to find the words. See how many you can find.

```
B R E A D C H
U A G P A O A
T I G P T O M
T S E L E K E
E I P E A I A
R N F I G E T
M I L K N U T
```

1. _____   8. _____

2. _____   9. _____

3. _____   10. _____

4. _____   11. _____

5. _____   12. _____

6. _____   13. _____

7. _____   14. _____

Name _____

Word Square Puzzle 36

Below is a word square puzzle. It has 15 animal words hidden in it. You can go across and down to find the words. See how many you can find.

```
A G C A T O E
F O W L I O N
O A P I G L A
X T O H E N M
D U C K R A T
W O L F A P E
M U L E D O G
```

1. _____   9. _____

2. _____   10. _____

3. _____   11. _____

4. _____   12. _____

5. _____   13. _____

6. _____   14. _____

7. _____   15. _____

8. _____

Name _____

Word Square Puzzle 37

Below is a word square puzzle. It has 12 things to wear in it. You can go across and down to find the words. See how many you can find.

```
S  K  I  R  T  D  S
H  G  C  L  R  R  H
I  L  S  H  O  E  O
R  O  L  A  B  S  R
T  V  I  T  E  S  T
K  E  P  A  N  T  S
C  A  P  E  B  O  W
```

1. _____   7. _____

2. _____   8. _____

3. _____   9. _____

4. _____   10. _____

5. _____   11. _____

6. _____   12. _____

Name _____

Word Square Puzzle 38

Below is a word square puzzle. It has nine descriptive words hidden in it.
You can go across and down to find the words. See how many you can find.

```
O  I  L  Y  S  B
G  O  O  D  A  A
A  O  C  O  L  D
M  E  H  O  T  R
S  P  I  C  Y  Y
B  U  R  N  T  W
```

1. _____   6. _____

2. _____   7. _____

3. _____   8. _____

4. _____   9. _____

5. _____

Name _____

Word Square Puzzle 39

Below is a word square puzzle. It has nine words that tell you how things can feel when you touch them. You can go across and down to find the words. See how many you can find.

```
D  E  S  O  F  T
A  E  M  D  R  Y
M  R  O  U  G  H
P  C  O  L  D  A
W  E  T  I  O  R
A  E  H  O  T  D
```

1. _____   6. _____

2. _____   7. _____

3. _____   8. _____

4. _____   9. _____

5. _____

Name _____

Word Square Puzzle 40

Below is a Hunting Square. If you follow the directions carefully, you will track down the animal that escaped from the zoo.

```
A  F  A  R  M  S
P  L  G  O  G  R
S  T  R  E  E  T
S  T  O  P  I  T
R  O  C  D  I  P
B  A  K  E  S  C
```

Directions: The last word of each clue is hidden in the puzzle above. Each clue below helps you find a letter of the animal that escaped from the zoo. Read each clue carefully and then put the letters together to find the animal.

Clues:

1. Go to the end of **street**.   _____

2. Look in the center of **pit**.   _____

3. Look at what is above **rock**.   _____

4. Look at the end of **tree**.   _____

5. Look in the middle of **farms**.   _____

Answer: _____

Name _____

Word Square Puzzle 41

Below is a word square puzzle. It has seven words that tell how you may feel when you are having fun. You can go across and down to find the words. See how many you can find.

```
A M J O L L Y
L E L C C A H
B R I G H T A
G R V E E O P
L Y E Y E O P
A M L E R R Y
D E Y A Y O E
```

1. _____   5. _____

2. _____   6. _____

3. _____   7. _____

4. _____

108

Name _____

Word Square Puzzle 42

Below is a word square puzzle. It has 12 words that tell how you may feel when you are **not** having fun. You can go across and down to find words. See how many you can find.

```
U N H A P P Y W
N L E G M A D R
J O Y L E S S E
S W D O W N A T
O U B O R E D C
U A R M E A N H
R E A Y O U R E
U N L U C K Y D
```

1. _____   7. _____

2. _____   8. _____

3. _____   9. _____

4. _____   10. _____

5. _____   11. _____

6. _____   12. _____

© Fearon Teacher Aids FE7966
Reproducible

Name _____

Word Riddle Puzzle 43

Below are six clues for six words. First figure out each word from the clue and write it in the space provided. When you put the first letter of each word together, you will have an animal that will have something in it to help you unlock your door.

1. I'm a female deer. _____

2. I'm a very strong animal. _____

3. I'm a sound a horse makes. _____

4. I'm an animal with a pouch. _____

5. I'm an animal that has a trunk. _____

6. I'm the day before today. _____

____ ____ ____ ____ ____ ____

Name _____

Word Riddle Puzzle 44

Below are six clues for six words. First figure out each word from the clue and write it in the space provided. When you put the first letter of each word together, you will have a very important person.

1. I'm an insect.   _____

2. I'm the opposite of **in**.   _____

3. I mean the same as **story**.   _____

4. I mean the same as **aid**.   _____

5. I'm the opposite of **begin**.   _____

6. Cars ride on me.   _____

____ ____ ____ ____ ____ ____

111

Name _____

Word Riddle Puzzle 45

Below are five clues for five words. First figure out each word from the clue and write it in the space provided. When you put the first letter of each word together, you will know what has lots of keys but can't open anything.

1. I'm what you have if something hurts you. _____

2. I'm another word for **sick**. _____

3. I'm a relative. _____

4. I'm part of your finger. _____

5. I'm the opposite of **young**. _____

_____ _____ _____ _____ _____

Name _____

Word Riddle Puzzle 46

Below are six clues for six words. First figure out each word from the clue and write it in the space provided. When you put the first letter of each word together, you will have the answer to this riddle:
What grows smaller the longer it stays?

1. I'm what you do on a stove.   _____

2. I'm the opposite of **question**.   _____

3. I'm part of your face.   _____

4. I'm the opposite of **light**.   _____

5. I'm also part of your face.   _____

6. I'm what you do when you are hungry. _____

____ ___ ___ ___ ___ ___

Name _____

Word Riddle Puzzle 47

Each sentence below gives you a clue to a letter. Put the letters together and you will have the answer to this riddle:
What howls and whistles but has no voice?

_____ 1. Its first letter is in **twist**, but not in **this**.

_____ 2. Its second letter is in **drive**, but not in **drove**.

_____ 3. Its third letter is in **twin**, but not in **twist**.

_____ 4. Its fourth letter is in **bind**, but not in **blink**.

_____ _____ _____ _____

Word Riddle Puzzle 48

Each sentence below gives you a clue to a letter. Put the letters together and you will have the answer to this riddle:
What never moves but goes up, down, and turns?

_____ 1. Its first letter is in **cart**, but not in **cat**.

_____ 2. Its second letter is in **boat**, but not in **beat**.

_____ 3. Its third letter is in **bake**, but not in **bike**.

_____ 4. Its fourth letter is in **bead**, but not in **beat**.

_____ _____ _____ _____

Name _____

Word Riddle Puzzle 49

Each sentence below gives you a clue to a letter. Put the letters together and you will have the answer to this riddle:
What has a mouth but never eats?

_____ 1. Its first letter is in **fire**, but not in **fine**.

_____ 2. Its second letter is in **nine**, but not in **name**.

_____ 3. Its third letter is in **live**, but not in **life**.

_____ 4. Its fourth letter is in **fake**, but not in **faking**.

_____ 5. Its fifth letter is in **park**, but not in **pack**.

____ ____ ____ ____ ____

Word Riddle Puzzle 50

Each sentence below gives you a clue to a letter. Put the letters together and you will have the answer to this riddle:
What has lots of eyes but doesn't see?

_____ 1. Its first letter is in **lap**, but not in **late**.

_____ 2. Its second letter is in **boat**, but not in **beat**.

_____ 3. Its third letter is in **note**, but not in **honey**.

_____ 4. Its fourth letter is in **band**, but not in **bend**.

_____ 5. Its fifth letter is in **feet**, but not in **fame**.

_____ 6. Its sixth letter is in **grow**, but not in **grew**.

____ ____ ____ ____ ____ ____

Name _____

Word Riddle Puzzle 51

Each sentence below gives you a clue to a letter. Put the letters together and you will have the answer to this riddle: What small thing never runs out of light in the night?

_____ 1. Its first letter is in **fall**, but not in **tall**.

_____ 2. Its second letter is in **time**, but not in **tame**.

_____ 3. Its third letter is in **barn**, but not in **band**.

_____ 4. Its fourth letter is in **bake**, but not in **baking**.

_____ 5. Its fifth letter is in **fan**, but not in **tan**.

_____ 6. Its sixth letter is in **sled**, but not in **stayed**.

_____ 7. Its seventh letter is in **buy**, but not in **bus**.

_____ _____ _____ _____ _____ _____

Name _____

Word Riddle Puzzle 52

Each sentence below gives you a clue to a letter. Put the letters together and you will have the answer to this riddle: What has a head but does not think?

_____ 1. Its first letter is in **table**, but not in **bathe**.

_____ 2. Its second letter is in **fell**, but not in **fall**.

_____ 3. Its third letter is in **plant**, but not in **plane**.

_____ 4. Its fourth letter is in **cut**, but not in **cup**.

_____ 5. Its fifth letter is in **butter**, but not in **batter**.

_____ 6. Its sixth letter is in **piece**, but not in **pipes**.

_____ 7. Its seventh letter is in **west**, but not in **twist**.

_____ _____ _____ _____ _____ _____

Name _____

Rhyming Word Puzzles 53

Below are some clues. Each clue will help you figure out the word it refers to. Hint: All the words rhyme.

1. This is the opposite of **fat**. _____

2. This holds things together. _____

3. A fish has this. _____

4. This is part of your face. _____

5. This is what you try to do when you
   play a game. _____

6. This can hold or store things. _____

Name _____

Rhyming Word Puzzles 54

Below are some clues. Each clue will help you figure out the word it refers to. Hint: All the words rhyme.

1. You use this to call someone.   _____

2. You make this sound when something
   hurts you.   _____

3. This is a part of the body that you
   can break.   _____

4. Pine trees have this.   _____

5. You can get this from a bank.   _____

6. This is a male bee.   _____

Name _____

Rhyming Word Puzzles 55

Below are some clues. Each clue will help you figure out the word it refers to. Hint: All the words rhyme.

1. You do this to your hair.   _____

2. You live here.   _____

3. This is a large round roof.   _____

4. A car may be trimmed with this.   _____

5. This is a city in Italy.   _____

6. This is a folktale person.   _____

Name _____

Rhyming Word Puzzles 56

Below are some clues. Each clue will help you figure out the word it refers to. Hint: All the words rhyme.

1. You say this to quiet someone.   _____

2. You do this when you are in a hurry.   _____

3. This is partly melted snow.   _____

4. You do this when you squeeze
   something together.   _____

5. This is a command given to a
   sled-drawn dog team.   _____

6. You do this when your cheeks get red.   _____

Name _____

Rhyming Word Puzzles 57

Below are some clues. Each clue will help you figure out the word it refers to. Hint: All the words rhyme.

1. You do this in a chair.   _____

2. You want your clothes to do this.   _____

3. You do this to a ball.   _____

4. You use this glove in baseball.   _____

5. This is a large hole.   _____

6. You do this to wool.   _____

7. This is a small amount of something. _____

Name _____

Rhyming Word Puzzles 58

Below are some clues. Each clue will help you figure out the word it refers to. Hint: All the words rhyme.

1. You use this to cool yourself. _____

2. Your father is this. _____

3. The sun can do this to you. _____

4. You put things in this. _____

5. You did this when you were in a rush. _____

6. You cook in this. _____

7. This is a boy's name. _____

Name _____

Rhyming Word Puzzles 59

Below are some clues. Each clue will help you figure out the word it refers to. Hint: All the words rhyme.

1. You like to play this.   _____

2. This is the opposite of **wild**.   _____

3. You have this if you are well-known.   _____

4. This is the opposite of **different**.   _____

5. You may be this if you hurt your leg.   _____

6. This comes from fire.   _____

7. This tells who you are.   _____

Name _____

Rhyming Word Puzzles 60

Below are some clues. Each clue will help you figure out the word it refers to. Hint: All the words rhyme.

1. You bounce this. _____

2. This is part of a room. _____

3. This is found in a house. _____

4. This is the opposite of **short**. _____

5. You do this when you phone. _____

6. This is a large shopping center. _____

7. An animal is kept in this. _____

Name _____

Rhyming Word Puzzles 61

The answers for each of the following clues are two rhyming words.

Example: amusing rabbit   Answer: funny bunny

1. best dad   _____ _____

2. heavy mouse chaser   _____ _____

3. high fence   _____ _____

4. comfortable insect   _____ _____

Name _____

Rhyming Word Puzzles 62

The answers for each of the following clues are two rhyming words.

Example: dairy knife   Answer: butter   cutter

1. large hog   _____   _____

2. damp animal   _____   _____

3. foolish horse   _____   _____

4. cross royal lady   _____   _____

Name _____

Rhyming Word Puzzles 63

The answers for each of the following clues are two rhyming words.

Example: unhappy boy   Answer: sad   lad

1. something you just bought
   to wear on your foot   _____   _____

2. little scarf   _____   _____

3. dual difficulty   _____   _____

4. small boxed goodies   _____   _____

Name _____

Rhyming Word Puzzles 64

The answers for each of the following clues are two rhyming words.

1. ill fowl   _____   _____

2. old story   _____   _____

3. peculiar whiskers   _____   _____

4. boring bird   _____   _____

Rhyming Word Puzzles 65

The answers for each of the following clues are two rhyming words.

1. large music group   _____   _____

2. head robber   _____   _____

3. pleasant little animals that
   eat cheese   _____   _____

4. blonde locks   _____   _____

Name _____

Scrambled Word Puzzles 66

Two words are put together to make a scrambled set. The letters for each word in the scrambled set are given in order, but the words are mixed together. A clue is given for each set. The first is done for you.

1. two farm animals   hceown   _____hen_____ _____cow_____

2. two house animals   dcoagt   _____ _____

3. two wild animals   faopxe   _____ _____

4. two colors   rgereden   _____ _____

5. two fruits   papeplare   _____ _____

Name _____

Scrambled Word Puzzles 67

Two words are put together to make a scrambled set. The letters for each word in the scrambled set are given in order, but the words are mixed together. A clue is given for each set.

1. two writing things   ppaedn   _____ _____

2. two things to wear   hsoactk   _____ _____

3. two drinks   jmuiiclek   _____ _____

4. two insects   maontth   _____ _____

5. two pets   hdamostger   _____ _____

© Fearon Teacher Aids FE7966
Reproducible

Name _____

Scrambled Word Puzzles 68

Two words are put together to make a scrambled set. The letters for each word in the scrambled set are given in order, but the words are mixed together. A clue is given for each set.

1. two boys' names   msatrevke   _____ _____

2. two girls' names   csaharrooln   _____ _____

3. two dairy foods   mbiutltekr   _____ _____

4. two games   thenocnkiesy   _____ _____

5. two months   jmaurnech   _____ _____

Name _____

Scrambled Word Puzzles 69

Here are six words—each with a clue. Change the letters of each word so that they fit the clue for a new word. The first is done for you.

1. was: You use this to cut down a tree. _____saw_____

2. raw: This is the opposite of **peace**. _____

3. tip: This is a large hole. _____

4. not: This is a heavy weight _____

5. now: The opposite of **lost**. _____

6. sag: A car needs this to run. _____

© Fearon Teacher Aids FE7966
Reproducible

Name _____

Scrambled Word Puzzles 70

Here are six words—each with a clue. Change the letters of each word so that they fit the clue for a new word. The first is done for you.

1. but: You bathe in this.　　　　_____tub_____

2. nip: This has a point.　　　　_____

3. mad: This holds back water.　　_____

4. pea: This is a wild animal.　　_____

5. leaf: This is an insect.　　　_____

6. shore: This animal eats hay.　_____

Name _____

Scrambled Word Puzzles 71

Here are six words—each with a clue. Change the letters of each word so that they fit the clue for a new word. The first is done for you.

1. grin: You wear this on your finger.   _____ring_____

2. dear: This is something you do to a book.   _____

3. life: You do this to your nails.   _____

4. rare: This means **in the back**.   _____

5. lame: This is a man.   _____

6. late: This is a story.   _____

© Fearon Teacher Aids FE7966

Name _____

Scrambled Word Puzzles 72

Here are six words—each with a clue. Change the letters of each word so that they fit the clue for a new word. The first is done for you.

1. hint: This is the opposite of **fat**.   _____thin_____

2. name: This is part of a horse.   _____

5. paws: This is an insect.   _____

4. deal: A pencil has this.   _____

5. fowl: This is a wild animal.   _____

6. mile: This is a fruit.   _____

Name _____

Scrambled Word Puzzles 73

Here are six words—each with a clue. Change the letters of each word so that they fit the clue for a new word.

1. mean: This tells who you are. _____

2. save: This holds flowers. _____

3. take: This is a girl's name. _____

4. sole: You don't want to do this in a game. _____

5. more: This is a city in Italy. _____

6. lamp: This is a tree. _____

Name _____

Scrambled Word Puzzles 74

Below are sentences with a word, a letter, and a clue. Put the word and letter together and you will have the answer to the clue. You can rearrange the letters in any way. The first is done for you.

1. **No** plus **e** equals a number. _____one_____

2. **On** plus **w** equals what you did when you beat the other team. _____

3. **As** plus **e** equals an ocean. _____

4. **Ow** plus **t** equals a number. _____

5. **To** plus **e** equals part of your foot. _____

Name _____

Scrambled Word Puzzles 75

Below are sentences with a word, a letter, and a clue. Put the word and letter together and you will have the answer to the clue. You can rearrange the letters in any way. The first is done for you.

1. **Dear** plus **b** equals what a man can grow
   on his face.   _____beard_____

2. **Beak** plus **r** equals what happens to
   glasses when they fall.   _____

3. **Sow** plus **h** equals something you
   can watch.   _____

4. **Pie** plus **r** equals what a fruit is when it
   is fully developed.   _____

5. **Salt** plus **b** equals a loud noise.   _____

Name _____

Scrambled Word Puzzles 76

Below are sentences with a word, two letters, and a clue. Put the word and letters together and you will have the answer to the clue. You can rearrange the letters in any way.

1. **Ear** plus **m** and **d** equals what you do when you sleep. _____

2. **Hear** plus **c** and **s** equals what you do when you look for someone or something. _____

3. **Bale** plus **c** and **h** equals something that gets clothes white. _____

4. **Soar** plus **b** and **b** equals what a towel does. _____

Name _____

Hidden Word Puzzles 77

Find the word that is hidden in each sentence. The words following the sentence will tell you what to look for. Hint: The answer may be hidden in one or more words of the sentence. The first is done for you.

1. I spent some time at the fair. (something you write with)

   <u>s**pen**t—pen</u>

2. I have a pretty dresser in my room. (something a girl wears)

   _____

3. I put my clothing in my drawer. (something that is fun to do)

   _____

4. I drink a lot of milk. (something that a pen needs)

   _____

Name _____

Hidden Word Puzzles 78

Find the word that is hidden in each sentence. The words following the sentence will tell you what to look for. Hint: The answer may be hidden in one or more words of the sentence. The first is done for you.

1. I can dye my dress blue. (something sweet)   **can dy**e—candy

2. I play on the baseball team. (a drink)   _____

3. The goats butt Eric in the back.
   (a dairy food)   _____

4. I have finished three problems so far.
   (something to sit on)   _____

Hidden Word Puzzles 79

Find the word that is hidden in each sentence. The words following the sentence will tell you what to look for. Hint: The answer may be hidden in one or more words of the sentence.

1. I like to wear pants. (an insect)   _____

2. When are we going to the party?
   (a farm animal)   _____

3. I was pleased to see her. (an insect)   _____

4. I do very well in school. (a bird)   _____

Name _____

Hidden Word Puzzles 80

Find the word that is hidden in each sentence. The words following the sentence will tell you what to look for. Hint: The answer may be hidden in one or more words of the sentence.

1. My mother is coming to school today. (an insect) _____

2. I like to wear a cape. (a wild animal) _____

3. The bird's plumes are colorful. (a fruit) _____

4. Please eat your broth, Ernest. (a relative) _____

Hidden Word Puzzles 81

Find the name of the vegetable that is hidden in each sentence. Hint: The answer may be hidden in one or more words of the sentence.

1. Mary will speak to the class. _____

2. The beetles were eating our leaves. _____

3. She will be an animal in the play. _____

4. The sun made our car rot. _____

Name _____

Hidden Word Puzzles 82

Find the name of the school subject that is hidden in each sentence.
Hint: The answer may be hidden in one or more words of the sentence.

1. I will read in George's house. _____

2. The mat had some dirt on it. _____

3. Please give this to Ryan. _____

4. In the story, the germ and the medicine
   fought a battle. _____

5. The cartoon made us laugh a lot. _____

Name _____

Hidden Clue Puzzles 83

Below are six clues for six words. Each word cannot lose because it has **win** in it. The first is done for you.

1. This win is a season.   ___winter___

2. This win is part of a bird.   _____

3. This win is something you can look through.   _____

4. This win is something you can do with
   your eyes.   _____

5. This win is something older people
   may drink.   _____

6. This win can make a breeze.   _____

Name _____

Hidden Clue Puzzles 84

Below are six clues for six words. Each word weighs a lot because it has a **ton** in it.

1. A sweater may have these.   _____

2. This holds things.   _____

3. The name of the first President.   _____

4. You have this in your throat.   _____

5. You have this in your mouth.   _____

6. This is very soft.   _____

Name _____

Hidden Clue Puzzles 85

Below are eight clues for eight words. Each word can take you for a ride because it has a **car** in it.

1. This car is a vegetable. _____

2. This car will take a baby for a ride. _____

3. This car is a four-letter word that holds things. _____

4. This car is something that you can write on. _____

5. This car is the opposite of **neglect**. _____

6. This car is what you need to get on a
bus or taxi. _____

7. This car is something you can walk on. _____

8. This car is a girl's name. _____

Name _____

Hidden Clue Puzzles 86

Below are 10 clues for 10 words. Each word has an **ant** in it.

1. You wear these.   _____

2. This grows in the ground.   _____

3. You do this to your paper when you
   write in cursive.   _____

4. This is an animal with horns.   _____

5. This lights up the night.   _____

6. This is a very dangerous animal.   _____

7. You do this when you breathe quickly.   _____

8. A deer has these.   _____

9. This is a former president's name.   _____

10. This is found on the head of insects.   _____

Name _____

Hidden Clue Puzzles 87

Below are 10 clues for 10 words. Each word must have a beginning because it has an **end** in it.

1. You do this when you bow.   _____

2. You do this when you sew something

   that is torn.   _____

3. You may have done this when someone

   needed something that you had.   _____

4. A car has this.   _____

5. You do this when you take care of someone. _____

6. You do this when you mix things together.   _____

7. Something soft would be this.   _____

8. A pal is this.   _____

9. A monster is also this.   _____

10. You do this when you praise someone.   _____

Name _____

Hidden Clue Puzzles 88

Below are five clues for five animals. After you figure out each animal, you will be able to solve the puzzle.

1. I'm very large and heavy and carry all my things with me. What am I and how do I carry my things?

   _____   _____

2. I live in the water and I like to weigh myself a lot. What am I and why do I like to weigh myself a lot?

   _____   _____

3. I'm a rather large rodent who sews a lot. What am I and why do I sew a lot?

   _____   _____

4. I'm a very proud bird and I keep myself looking good all the time. What am I and why do I keep myself looking fine all the time?

   _____   _____

5. I'm large and can hop very fast. I take my baby with me wherever I go. What am I and why do I take my baby with me?

   _____   _____

Diagnostic Checklist for Vocabulary Development in a Balanced Reading Program (Primary Grades).

Student's Name:

Grade:

Teacher:

	Yes	No	Sometimes
1. The child shows that he or she is developing a vocabulary consciousness by recognizing that some words have more than one meaning.			
2. The child uses context clues to figure out word meanings.			
3. The child can state the opposite of words, such as *stop, tall, fat, long, happy, big*.			
4. The child can state the synonym of words, such as *big, heavy, thin, mean, fast, hit*.			
5. The child can state different meanings for homographs. Examples: I did not *state* what *state* I live in. Do not *roll* the *roll* on the floor. *Train* your dog not to bark when it hears a *train*.			
6. The child is developing a vocabulary of the senses by being able to state words that describe various sounds, smells, sights, tastes, and touches.			
7. The child is expanding his or her vocabulary by combining two words to form compound words, such as *grandfather, bedroom, cupcake, backyard, toothpick, buttercup*.			
8. The child is expanding his or her vocabulary by combining roots of words with prefixes and suffixes. Examples are *return, friendly, unhappy, disagree, dirty, precook, unfriendly*.			
9. The child is able to give the answer to a number of word riddles.			
10. The child is able to make up a number of word riddles.			
11. The child is able to classify various objects, such as fruits, animals, colors, pets.			
12. The child is able to give words that are associated with certain objects and ideas. Example: hospital—*nurse, doctor, beds, sick persons, medicine*.			
13. The child is able to complete some analogy proportions, such as *happy* is to *sad* as *big* is to _____.			
14. The child shows that he or she is developing a vocabulary consciousness by using the dictionary to look up unknown words.			

Answers

Answers to Skill 1

Practice 1 (p. 26)
1. play   4. suit
2. box   5. point
3. rose

Practice 2 (p. 27)
1. pitch   4. rest
2. run   5. bear
3. strike

Practice 3 (p. 28)
1. plant   4. lamb
2. plum   5. iron
3. monkey

Practice 4 (p. 29)
1. break   4. pinch
2. broke   5. fast
3. flowed

Practice 5 (p. 30)
1. sad   4. good
2. silly   5. tired
3. sick

Practice 6 (p. 31)
1. angry   4. ashamed
2. proud   5. happy
3. insulted

Practice 7 (p. 32)
1. embarrassed   4. guilty
2. scared   5. peculiar
3. joyful

Practice 8 (p. 33)
1. hard   4. cure
2. not believable   5. rough
3. double

Practice 9 (p. 34)
1. gentle
2. well-known
3. large, huge

4. wide
5. wild, savage
6. large, big
7. brave, courageous
8. powerful, strong
9. destroyed
10. equal

Practice 10 (p. 35)
Possible answers:
1. play   6. zoo
2. boat   7. did
3. hen   8. swim
4. week   9. Fruit
5. friend   10. park

Practice 11 (p. 36)
Possible answers:
1. Jack   6. do
2. walk   7. Carol
3. school   8. cat
4. baseball 9. circus
5. swimming 10. dog

Practice 12 (p. 37)
1. mouse   7. cheese
2. in   8. play
3. is   9. hide
4. smart   10. seek
5. it   11. the
6. give   12. house

Practice 13 (p. 38)
1. was   11. tree
2. tree   12. night
3. cat   13. morning
4. branch   14. she
5. sat   15. not
6. sat   16. what
7. sat   17. we
8. to   18. loud
9. down   19. my
10. meow   20. ran

Practice 14 (p. 39)
1. shy   9. never
2. am   10. speak
3. No   11. not
4. me   12. be
5. what   13. very
6. say   14. have
7. school   15. friends
8. hand

Practice 15 (p. 40)
1. cookie   16. no
2. little   17. Look
3. had   18. at
4. big   19. looked
5. tail   20. cookie
6. girl   21. talking
7. as   22. eat
8. was   23. the
9. bunny   24. table
10. say   25. hopped
11. not   26. ran
12. eat   27. but
13. do   28. catch
14. me   29. bunny
15. girl   30. fast

Answers to Skill 2

Practice 1 (p. 46)
1. big   4. bright
2. ill   5. handsome
3. joyful

Practice 2 (p. 47)
1. little   4. lady
2. correct   5. thin
3. mean

Practice 3 (p. 48)
1. price   4. struck
2. pal   5. place
3. rip

Practice 4 (p. 49)

1. wealthy
2. bright
3. moist
4. healthy
5. finish

Practice 5 (p. 50)

1. clever
2. start
3. chum
4. head
5. aid
6. end
7. defend
8. scent
9. damage
10. trouble

Practice 6 (p. 51)

1. tall
2. little
3. low
4. later
5. back

Practice 7 (p. 52)

1. well
2. good
3. clean
4. beautiful
5. asleep

Practice 8 (p. 53)

1. sad
2. empty
3. old
4. stale
5. guilty

Practice 9 (p. 54)

1. tall, short
2. rough, soft
3. win, lose
4. rises, sets
5. wet, dry

Practice 10 (p. 55)

Possible answers:

1. You may <u>laugh</u> when you are <u>happy</u>, and you may <u>cry</u> when you are <u>sad</u>.
2. You are usually <u>awake</u> during the <u>day</u>, and you are usually <u>asleep</u> during the <u>night</u>.
3. You are <u>strong</u> when you are <u>healthy</u>, and you are <u>weak</u>

when you are <u>sick</u>.

4. When you are <u>kind</u>, people <u>love</u> you, but when you are <u>cruel</u>, people <u>hate</u> you.
5. My <u>sister</u> is <u>always</u> late, but my <u>brother</u> is <u>never</u> late.

Answers to Skill 3

Practice 1 (p. 61)

1. bark
2. train
3. fall
4. pet

Practice 2 (p. 62)

1. spring
2. well
3. plant
4. fan

Practice 3 (p. 63)

1. groom
2. park
3. grade
4. fair

Practice 4 (p. 64)

1. show
2. fine
3. spell
4. hit
5. band

Practice 5 (p. 65)

1. rose
2. hose
3. point
4. jack
5. run

Practice 6 (p. 66)

1. duck
2. pin
3. coat
4. mine

Practice 7 (p. 67)

1. ruler
2. flag
3. ball
4. shrimp
5. line
6. top
7. block
8. slip
9. bank

Practice 8 (p. 68)

1. shake
2. mean
3. bridge
4. tape
5. box
6. chief
7. one
8. play

Practice 9 (p. 69)

1. change
2. seal
3. float
4. fly
5. bowl
6. letters
7. walk
8. slip

Practice 10 (p. 70)

1. tie
2. glasses
3. ring
4. rest
5. pitcher
6. study
7. tube
8. stamp
9. kid
10. crane
11. key
12. snap

Answers to Fun with Words

Word Riddles 1 (p. 74)

1. cow
2. duck
3. hen
4. horse

Word Riddles 2 (p. 75)

1. pig
2. dog
3. mule
4. goose

Word Riddles 3 (p. 76)

1. monkey
2. deer
3. lion
4. tiger

Word Riddles 4 (p. 77)

1. fox
2. wolf
3. bear
4. panther

Word Riddles 5 (p. 78)

1. start–star
2. rain–train
3. read–bread
4. play–lay

© Fearon Teacher Aids FE7966

Word Riddles 6 (p. 79)

1. bowl–owl   3. lass–glass
2. late–plate   4. bee–beetle

Word Riddles 7 (p. 80)

1. plant–ant   3. beep–bee
2. chill–ill   4. doe–dove

Word Riddles 8 (p. 81)

1. ride–bride
2. room–groom
3. moth–mother
4. fat–father

Word Riddles 9 (p. 82)

1. clock–lock   3. rake–brake
2. soil–spoil   4. pear–pearl

Word Riddles 10 (p. 83)

1. oar–board   3. drug–rug
2. rob–robe   4. rag–brag

Word Riddles 11 (p. 84)

1. cram–cramp
2. host–ghost
3. wren–wrench
4. sill–silly

Word Riddles 12 (p. 85)

1. cab–in–cabin
2. rob–in–robin
3. pal–ace–palace
4. pan–try–pantry

Word Riddles 13 (p. 86)

1. car–ton–carton
2. arm–or–armor
3. cup–board–cupboard
4. cot–ton–cotton

Word Riddles 14 (p. 87)

1. orange   3. bark
2. train   4. park

Word Riddles 15 (p. 88)

1. root   3. crown
2. jam   4. ruler

Word Riddles 16 (p. 89)

1. bridge   3. pit
2. blocks   4. band

Word Puzzels 17 (p. 90)

1. barn   6. nice, kind
2. burn   7. sick
3. rake   8. blue
4. game   9. wolf
5. sled   10. duck

Word Puzzles 18 (p. 91)

1. dad   6. pop
2. tot   7. nun
3. bib   8. gag
4. mom   9. pup
5. sis   10. eye

Word Puzzles 19 (p. 92)

1. cat   4. thread
2. ate   5. add
3. teeth

Word Puzzles 20 (p. 92)

1. pal   4. arithmetic
2. alone   5. ice
3. near   6. cent

Word Puzzles 21 (p. 93)

1. book   5. house
2. key   6. ear
3. yellow   7. rose
4. wash

Word Puzzles 22 (p. 94)

1. prince   5. girl
2. end   6. left
3. day   7. take
4. young

Word Puzzles 23 (p. 95)

1. goat (oat)
2. scream (cream)
3. hammer (ham)
4. pearl (pea, pear)

Word Puzzles 24 (p. 95)

1. chair (hair)
2. tear (ear)
3. farm (arm)
4. chestnut (chest)

Word Puzzles 25 (p. 95)

1. honey (one)
2. often (ten)
3. freight (eight)
4. attend (ten)

Word Puzzles 26 (p. 96)

1. a   4. mane
2. ma   5. Maine
3. man

Word Puzzles 27 (p. 96)

1. I   4. thin
2. hi   5. think
3. hit

Word Puzzles 28 (p. 97)

1. food   5. told
2. good   6. toll
3. gold   7. roll
4. cold   8. role

Word Puzzles 29 (p. 98)

1. match   5. patch
2. catch   6. pitch
3. hatch   7. witch
4. latch   8. watch

Word Puzzles 30 (p. 99)

1. a   5. enter
2. be   6. father
3. cup, can   7. garbage
4. dark

Word Puzzles 31 (p. 99)

1. ace
2. add
3. bee
4. off
5. age
6. she
7. pin

Word Puzzles 32 (p. 100)

1. roar
2. toast
3. bulb
4. gong
5. high
6. rear

Word Puzzles 33 (p. 100)

1. noon
2. toot
3. peep
4. reader
5. deed

Word Square Puzzle 34 (p. 101)

Across: gray, red, brown, pink, blue, green, black
Down: orange, purple, yellow

Word Square Puzzle 35 (p. 102)

Across: bread, pea, fig, milk, nut
Down: butter, raisin, egg, apple, date, tea, cookie, ham, meat

Word Square Puzzle 36 (p. 103)

Across: cat, fowl, owl, lion, pig, hen, duck, rat, wolf, ape, mule, dog
Down: fox, goat, tiger

Word Square Puzzle 37 (p. 104)

Across: skirt, shoe, pants, cape, bow
Down: shirt, glove, slip, hat, robe, dress, shorts

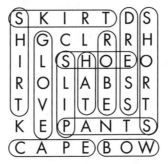

Word Square Puzzle 38 (p. 105)

Across: oily, good, cold, hot, spicy, burnt
Down: salty, bad, dry

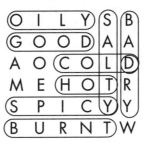

Word Square Puzzle 39 (p. 106)

Across: soft, dry, rough, cold, wet, hot
Down: damp, smooth, hard

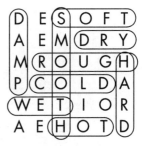

Word Square Puzzle 40 (p. 107)

1. T 2. I 3. G 4. E 5. R
Answer: TIGER

```
A F A Ⓡ M S
P L Ⓖ O G R
S T R E Ⓔ Ⓣ
S T O P Ⓘ T
R O C D I P
B A K E S C
```

Word Square Puzzle 41 (p. 108)

Across: jolly, bright
Down: glad, merry, lively, cheery, happy

```
A M J O L L Y
L E L C C A H
B R I G H T A
G R V E E O P
L Y E Y E R P
A M L E R R Y
D E Y A Y O E
```

155

Word Square
Puzzle 42 (p. 109)

Across: unhappy, mad, joyless, down, bored, mean, unlucky
Down: sour, low, gloomy, sad, wretched

Word Riddle
Puzzle 43 (p. 110)

1. doe   4. kangaroo
2. ox   5. elephant
3. neigh   6. yesterday
Answer: DONKEY

Word Riddle
Puzzle 44 (p. 111)

1. moth   4. help
2. out   5. end
3. tale   6. road
Answer: MOTHER

Word Riddle
Puzzle 45 (p. 112)

1. pain   4. nail
2. ill   5. old
3. aunt
Answer: PIANO

Word Riddle
Puzzle 46 (p. 113)

1. cook   4. dark
2. answer   5. lips
3. nose   6. eat
Answer: CANDLE

Word Riddle
Puzzle 47 (p. 114)

1. W   3. N
2. I   4. D
Answer: WIND

Word Riddle
Puzzle 48 (p. 114)

1. R   3. A
2. O   4. D
Answer: ROAD

Word Riddle
Puzzle 49 (p. 115)

1. R   4. E
2. I   5. R
3. V
Answer: RIVER

Word Riddle
Puzzle 50 (p. 115)

1. P   4. A
2. O   5. T
3. T   6. O
Answer: POTATO

Word Riddle
Puzzle 51 (p. 116)

1. F   5. F
2. I   6. L
3. R   7. Y
4. E
Answer: FIREFLY

Word Riddle
Puzzle 52 (p. 117)

1. L   5. U
2. E   6. C
3. T   7. E
4. T
Answer: LETTUCE

Rhyming Word
Puzzles 53 (p. 118)

1. thin   4. chin
2. pin   5. win
3. fin   6. bin, tin

Rhyming Word
Puzzles 54 (p. 119)

1. phone   4. cone
2. groan, moan   5. loan
3. bone   6. drone

Rhyming Word
Puzzles 55 (p. 120)

1. comb   4. chrome
2. home   5. Rome
3. dome   6. gnome

Rhyming Word
Puzzles 56 (p. 121)

1. hush   4. crush
2. rush   5. mush
3. slush   6. blush

Rhyming Word
Puzzles 57 (p. 122)

1. sit   5. pit
2. fit   6. knit
3. hit   7. bit
4. mitt

Rhyming Word
Puzzles 58 (p. 123)

1. fan   5. ran
2. man   6. pan
3. tan   7. Dan
4. can

Rhyming Word
Puzzles 59 (p. 124)

1. game   5. lame
2. tame   6. flame
3. fame   7. name
4. same

Rhyming Word Puzzles 60 (p. 125)

1. ball
2. wall
3. hall
4. tall
5. call
6. mall
7. stall

Rhyming Word Puzzles 61 (p. 126)

1. top pop
2. fat cat
3. tall wall
4. snug bug

Rhyming Word Puzzles 62 (p.127)

1. big pig
2. wet pet
3. silly filly
4. mean queen

Rhyming Word Puzzles 63 (p.128)

1. new shoe
2. small shawl
3. double trouble
4. snack pack

Rhyming Word Puzzles 64 (p. 129)

1. sick chick
2. stale tale
3. weird beard
4. dull gull

Rhyming Word Puzzles 65 (p. 129)

1. grand band
2. chief thief
3. nice mice
4. fair hair

Scrambled Word Puzzles 66 (p. 130)

1. hen, cow
2. dog, cat
3. fox, ape
4. red, green
5. pear, apple

Scrambled Word Puzzles 67 (p. 131)

1. pen, pad
2. hat, sock
3. juice, milk
4. moth, ant
5. hamster, dog

Scrambled Word Puzzles 68 (p. 132)

1. Mark, Steve
2. Carol, Sharon
3. milk, butter
4. tennis, hockey
5. June, March

Scrambled Word Puzzles 69 (p. 133)

1. saw
2. war
3. pit
4. ton
5. won
6. gas

Scrambled Word Puzzles 70 (p. 134)

1. tub
2. pin
3. dam
4. ape
5. flea
6. horse

Scrambled Word Puzzles 71 (p. 135)

1. ring
2. read
3. file
4. rear
5. male
6. tale

Scrambled Word Puzzles 72 (p. 136)

1. thin
2. mane
3. wasp
4. lead
5. wolf
6. lime

Scrambled Word Puzzles 73 (p. 137)

1. name
2. vase
3. Kate
4. lose
5. Rome
6. palm

Scrambled Word Puzzles 74 (p. 138)

1. one
2. won
3. sea
4. two
5. toe

Scrambled Word Puzzles 75 (p. 139)

1. beard
2. break
3. show
4. ripe
5. blast

Scrambled Word Puzzles 76 (p. 140)

1. dream
2. search
3. bleach
4. absorb

Hidden Word Puzzles 77 (p. 141)

1. spent—pen
2. dresser—dress
3. drawer—draw
4. drink—ink

Hidden Word Puzzles 78 (p. 142)

1. can dye—candy
2. team—tea
3. butt Eric—butter
4. so far—sofa

Hidden Word Puzzles 79 (p. 142)

1. p**ants**—ant
2. **Wh**en—hen
3. **was p**leased—wasp
4. **do ve**ry—dove

Hidden Word Puzzles 80 (p. 143)

1. **moth**er—moth
2. **cape**—ape
3. **plum**es—plum
4. **broth Er**nest—brother

Hidden Word Puzzles 81 (p. 143)

1. **spea**k—pea
2. **beet**les—beet
3. **be an**—bean
4. **car rot**—carrot

Hidden Word Puzzles 82 (p. 144)

1. **read in G**eorge's—reading
2. **mat h**ad—math
3. **t**his **to Ry**an—history
4. **germ an**d—German
5. **cart**oon—art

Hidden Clue Puzzles 83 (p. 145)

1. winter
2. wing
3. window
4. wink
5. wine
6. wind

Hidden Clue Puzzles 84 (p. 146)

1. button
2. carton
3. Washington
4. tonsils
5. tongue
6. cotton

Hidden Clue Puzzles 85 (p. 147)

1. carrot
2. carriage
3. cart
4. card
5. care
6. carfare
7. carpet
8. Carol

Hidden Clue Puzzles 86 (p. 148)

1. pants
2. plant
3. slant
4. antelope
5. lantern
6. panther
7. pant
8. antlers
9. Grant
10. antenna

Hidden Clue Puzzles 87 (p. 149)

1. bend
2. mend
3. lend
4. fender
5. tend
6. blend
7. tender
8. friend
9. fiend
10. commend

Hidden Clue Puzzles 88 (p. 150)

1. elephant—I have a trunk.
2. fish—I have scales
3. porcupine—I have lots of needles.
4. rooster—I have a comb.
5. kangaroo—I have a pouch.